YOUR recipe could appear in our next cookbook!

Share your tried & true family favorites with us instantly at

www.gooseberrypatch.com

If you'd rather jot 'em down by hand, just mail this form to...

Gooseberry Patch • Cookbooks – Call for Recipes
PO Box 812 • Columbus, OH 43216-0812

If your recipe is selected for a book, you'll receive a FREE copy!

Please share only your original recipes or those that you have made your own over the years.

Recipe Name:

Number of Servings:

Any fond memories about this recipe? Special touches you like to add or handy shortcuts?

Ingredients (include specific measurements):

Instructions (continue on back if needed):

Special Code: **cookbookspage**

T0026690

x

~ver

Extra space for recipe if needed:

Tell us about yourself...

Your complete contact information is needed so that we can send you your FREE cookbook, if your recipe is published. Phone numbers and email addresses are kept private and will only be used if we have questions about your recipe.

Name:

Address:

City: State: Zip:

Email:

Daytime Phone:

Thank you! Vickie & Jo Ann

Gooseberry Patch

•Secrets from•
GRANDMA'S
Kitchen

More than 200 delicious, tried & true recipes from grandmothers across the country, plus tips for making mealtime extra special.

GRANDMA'S PIES

HOME MADE

BAKED WITH LOVE

Gooseberry Patch

An imprint of Globe Pequot
64 South Main Street
Essex, CT 06426

www.gooseberrypatch.com

1•800•854•6673

Copyright 2023, Gooseberry Patch 978-1-62093-561-3

Do you have a tried & true recipe...

tip, craft or memory that you'd like to see featured in
a **Gooseberry Patch** cookbook? Visit our website at
www.gooseberrypatch.com and follow the
easy steps to submit your favorite family recipe.
Or send them to us at:

Gooseberry Patch
PO Box 812
Columbus, OH 43216-0812

Don't forget to include the number of servings your recipe makes,
plus your name, address, phone number and email address. If we
select your recipe, your name will appear right along with it...
and you'll receive a **FREE** copy of the book!

Contents

Dedication

For everyone who agrees that a scrumptious dish fixed "just like Grandma used to make" is almost as good as a warm hug from Grandma herself.

Appreciation

To all of our friends who shared your most treasured recipes from Grandma's recipe box, a sincere thanks!

Wake Up, *Sunshine!*

Overnight Crunch Coffee Cake

Leona Krivda
Belle Vernon, PA

Usually you wouldn't want your grandkids to have cake for breakfast. But once in awhile when they're at Momma's house won't hurt...and with a glass of milk, it's not all that bad, right?

2 c. all-purpose flour
1 t. baking powder
1 t. baking soda
1-1/2 t. cinnamon, divided
1/2 t. salt
2/3 c. butter, softened
1 c. sugar

1 c. brown sugar, packed
   and divided
2 eggs
1 c. buttermilk
1/4 t. nutmeg
1/2 c. chopped walnuts

In a bowl, whisk together flour, baking powder, baking soda, one teaspoon cinnamon and salt; set aside. In a separate large bowl, blend butter, sugar and 1/2 cup brown sugar until fluffy. Add eggs, one at a time, beating well after each. Add flour mixture to butter mixture alternately with buttermilk, beating well after each addition. Pour batter into a greased and floured 13"x9" baking pan. Combine remaining brown sugar, remaining cinnamon, nutmeg and nuts; sprinkle over batter. Cover with plastic wrap. Refrigerate overnight. Uncover; bake at 350 degrees for 30 to 35 minutes. Serve warm. Makes 10 to 12 servings.

Take time to enjoy a hearty family breakfast, just like Grandma's... warm biscuits with homemade jam, flapjacks with maple syrup, crisp bacon, sausage and farm-fresh eggs!

Wake up, *Sunshine!*

Granny's Hotcakes

Rex Dustman
Albany, OR

*This recipe was created by my Aunts Cecille and Roberta,
who both passed away years ago. It's a keeper!*

2 eggs
2 c. buttermilk
1/2 c. sour cream
2 t. baking soda
1 t. salt
1 c. cornmeal

1 c. all-purpose flour
1/2 c. old-fashioned oats,
   uncooked
1/3 c. sugar
3/4 t. baking powder

Beat eggs in a large bowl. Add buttermilk, sour cream, baking soda
and salt; beat well. Combine remaining ingredients in a separate bowl;
mix well and stir into egg mixture. Drop batter by 1/4 to 1/2 cupfuls
onto a griddle over medium heat. Turn over when bubbles appear
around the edges; cook until golden. Serves 4.

Brown Butter-Buttermilk Syrup

Lisa Langston
Conroe, TX

*An old-fashioned homemade syrup. Serve with waffles, pancakes,
French toast...even cake and ice cream! This syrup goes really well
with cinnamon cake and apples or pears.*

1/2 c. butter
3/4 c. sugar
1/2 c. buttermilk

1 t. baking soda
1 t. vanilla extract

In a small saucepan, melt butter over medium-low heat. Cook, swirling
occasionally, until butter turns dark golden. Skim off foam; remove
from heat. Pour into a bowl to stop the cooking, leaving any burned
sediment behind. Combine butter, sugar and buttermilk in a large
saucepan; mixture will bubble up. Cook over medium heat, whisking
until sugar dissolves. When mixture starts to boil, carefully whisk in
baking soda and vanilla. Cool; refrigerate syrup up to 2 weeks. Reheat
before serving. Serves 4 to 6.

Grandma Weidner's French Toast

Sarah Hente
Saint Charles, MO

My grandmother used to make this scrumptious breakfast for my siblings and me during the summers we spent on her and Grandpa's farm in rural Missouri.

2 c. milk
6 T. butter, sliced
1/4 c. brown sugar, packed
1 T. cinnamon
1 t. ground ginger

1 t. nutmeg
1 loaf brioche or challah bread,
  sliced 1/2-inch thick
Garnish: maple syrup, powdered
  sugar, sliced fruit

In a saucepan over low heat, combine milk, butter, brown sugar and spices. Cook, stirring occasionally, until butter is melted. Arrange bread slices on 2 greased baking sheets. With a pastry brush, brush milk mixture over both sides of bread slices, coating thoroughly. Bake, uncovered, at 325 degrees for 25 minutes, or until bread is crisp to the touch, yet still soft in the center. Serve garnished as desired. Makes 6 servings.

Cook up a yummy topping for pancakes and waffles.
Melt 2 tablespoons butter in a skillet over low heat. Stir in
1/4 cup brown sugar and 2 cups thinly sliced peaches.
Cook and stir until tender.

Wake up, *Sunshine!*

Amazing Overnight Waffles

Nancy Wolff
Bridgewater Corners, VT

This is an old family favorite that I have been making for years. It's perfect for when you have company, as you can mix up the batter the night before and it will be ready in the morning. Recipe can be easily doubled or tripled! These waffles also freeze well. Any leftover waffles I let cool on a baking rack and then wrap and place in the freezer. Perfect to pop in the toaster on a busy morning!

2 c. all-purpose flour	2 c. milk
1 t. active dry yeast	6 T. butter, melted
1 T. sugar	1 egg, beaten
1/2 t. salt	Garnish: favorite toppings

In a bowl, combine flour, yeast, sugar and salt. Add milk and whisk until blended. Cover bowl tightly with plastic wrap; let stand overnight at room temperature. In the morning, the batter will be bubbly on the surface. Add melted butter and egg to batter; beat well. Batter will be quite thin. Preheat a waffle iron; spray lightly with non-stick vegetable spray and rub on a little butter. Add one cup batter, or just enough to cover the cooking surface. Cook for 2 to 3 minutes, depending on waffle iron; do not overbake. Serve with your favorite toppings. Serves 3 to 4.

Don't waste one crumb of a scrumptious waffle! Before you add the batter to the waffle iron, brush it well with melted butter or vegetable oil. Then let the waffle cook until steam stops coming out the sides. The waffle will lift out easily.

Grandma's Skillet Cinnamon Rolls

Cyndy DeStefano
Mercer, PA

One of my most treasured things is my grandma's cast-iron skillet.
I love to cook in her skillet, because it takes me right back to
the days when I used to watch her cooking.

16-oz. pkg. hot roll mix
1/2 c. butter, softened
1 c. light brown sugar, packed
2 t. cinnamon

1 c. powdered sugar
2 T. milk
1 t. vanilla extract

Prepare hot roll mix as directed on package; let dough stand for
5 minutes. On a lightly floured surface, roll out dough into a 15-inch
by 10-inch rectangle. Spread with softened butter. Stir together brown
sugar and cinnamon; sprinkle over butter. Starting with one long side,
tightly roll up dough. Cut into 12 slices. Place rolls cut-side down in a
greased 12" cast-iron skillet. Cover loosely with plastic wrap and a tea
towel. Let rise for 30 minutes, or until rolls double in size. Uncover;
bake at 375 degrees for 20 to 25 minutes, until rolls are golden and
center rolls are done. Let cool in pan on a wire rack for 10 minutes.
Stir together powdered sugar, milk and vanilla; drizzle over rolls.
Makes one dozen.

Fresh flowers are a perfect pick-me-up at breakfast. A vintage teapot
makes a sweet vase for garden roses, daffodils or daisies.

Wake up, *Sunshine!*

Old-Fashioned Cocoa

Laura Lane
Carthage, MO

When I was a young child, my Grandma Mamie used to make homemade cocoa for me...now I make it for my own kids! My family just loves its rich flavor. I love it because it's so easy and I always have the ingredients on hand. My kids come running when they hear the sound the whisk makes in the pan. Read-aloud time is one of our favorite times to enjoy Old-Fashioned Cocoa together.

1/2 c. baking cocoa
1 c. sugar
1/2 c. cold water

1/2 gal. milk
Garnish: mini marshmallows
Optional: additional milk

In a large saucepan, whisk together cocoa and sugar until smooth. Add cold water; mix until smooth. Bring to a boil over medium heat. Continue to boil for about one minute, stirring constantly. Don't worry if mixture sticks to the sides of pan; it'll melt back into the cocoa as it heats up. Add milk. Cook and stir over medium heat, watching closely, until a mini marshmallow just starts to melt when added. If leaving unattended on stove, turn to the lowest heat. Serve with marshmallows and additional milk for cooling, if desired. Makes 8 servings.

Old-fashioned cinnamon toast is a sweet treat that's ready in a jiffy. Spread softened butter generously on one side of toasted bread, sprinkle with cinnamon-sugar and broil until hot and bubbly, one to 2 minutes. Perfect with a mug of hot cocoa!

Eggs for a Crowd

Mendy Purdome-Blomberg
Dixon, MO

Three generations of my family have enjoyed this recipe. I have wonderful memories of my grandparents preparing it during the holidays when everyone gathered at their home. It's great anytime you have overnight guests. Definitely a crowd-pleaser! Feel free to try different types of cheese, or add diced peppers for even more flavor. Grandma's secret...always choose the best-quality sausage for this dish.

8 slices white bread, cubed
1 lb. ground pork sausage,
   browned and drained
1/2 c. sliced mushrooms,
   drained if canned
1/2 c. shredded Cheddar cheese

1/2 c. shredded Swiss cheese
5 eggs
1-1/2 c. milk
1 T. Worcestershire sauce
1 t. mustard
salt and pepper to taste

Spray a 13"x9" baking pan with non-stick vegetable spray. Spread bread cubes in pan; pat sausage evenly over bread. Layer mushrooms and cheeses evenly over sausage; set aside. In a bowl, whisk together remaining ingredients; pour over cheeses. Cover and refrigerate overnight. In the morning, uncover; bake at 350 degrees for 40 minutes. Cut into squares and serve immediately. Serves 6 to 10.

Start a family reunion bright & early with a hearty breakfast gathering! Serve up all of Grandma's favorite breakfast treats... sure to bring back happy memories and inspire cheerful conversation.

Wake up, *Sunshine!*

Cottage Cheese Scrambled Eggs

Jill Valentine
Jackson, TN

Whenever I spent the night at her house in the country, Granny used to fix this for me with eggs from her own chickens. Delicious!

6 eggs
3/4 c. small-curd cottage cheese
2 T. milk
1 T. fresh chives, chopped

1/2 t. salt
1/8 t. pepper
2 T. butter

In a bowl, beat eggs lightly. Stir in cottage cheese, milk, chives, salt and pepper. Melt butter in a skillet over low heat; add egg mixture. Turn egg mixture with a spatula as it begins to thicken; do not stir. Cook just until set; serve immediately. Serves 4.

Pan-Fried Breakfast Potatoes

Ginny Watson
Scranton, PA

A must with eggs for breakfast! Here's a hint...don't stir the potatoes very much. Just let them cook, turning occasionally.

3 russet potatoes, peeled, cubed
   and rinsed

3 T. butter or bacon drippings
salt and pepper to taste

Pat potato cubes dry; set aside. Melt butter or drippings in a large skillet over medium heat. Add potatoes and stir to coat. Season with salt and pepper. Cover and cook for 10 minutes. Uncover and cook for another 10 minutes, turning often, until crisp and golden on all sides. Serves 3 to 4.

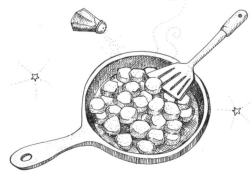

Leftover boiled potatoes make delicious hashbrowns. Toss a few extra potatoes in the pot at dinnertime to save for breakfast! Slice or dice and sauté until golden.

Cajun Breakfast Muffins

Brenda Melancon
McComb, MS

A long time ago during the Depression, my grandmother used to make this recipe. Folks then didn't have as many ingredients to choose from as now, but they got along by using what they had. I've updated it a bit to use newer ingredients, and they are still delicious. We Cajuns love to pour cane syrup over these muffins. Yum!

1 lb. ground pork breakfast
   sausage
2 c. biscuit baking mix
1/2 t. baking soda
1/2 c. shredded Cheddar cheese
1/4 c. green onion, chopped
1 egg, beaten
2/3 c. milk
1/8 t. hot pepper sauce

In a skillet over medium heat, lightly brown sausage, breaking apart into small pieces. Drain well; set aside. In a large bowl, whisk biscuit mix with baking soda. Add cheese and onion; stir well. In a small bowl, combine egg, milk and hot sauce. Add to biscuit mixture; stir until just combined. Fold in sausage. Place paper liners into a 12-cup muffin pan. Add 1/4 cup batter to each cup. Bake at 400 degrees for 25 to 30 minutes, until a wooden toothpick inserted in the center comes out clean. Makes 6 servings, 2 muffins each.

Grandmother could always be found wearing her apron...why not revive this useful tradition? Look through flea markets for some of the prettiest vintage aprons, or find a fun pattern and stitch one up in an afternoon.

Wake up, *Sunshine!*

Eggs à la Goldenrod

Irene Robinson
Cincinnati, OH

A hearty and pretty breakfast dish...very quick when you already have leftover hard-boiled eggs on hand. They're served in a white sauce, which as you'll see is really pretty easy to make.

4 eggs, hard-boiled, peeled
   and halved
2 T. all-purpose flour
1/4 t. salt

1/8 t. pepper
2 T. butter
1 c. milk
4 slices bread, toasted

Separate egg whites from yolks. Dice whites; crumble yolks and set aside. Mix together flour, salt and pepper in a small bowl; set aside. Melt butter in a saucepan over medium-low heat; add flour mixture and stir thoroughly. Slowly add milk and stir constantly until thick, about 2 minutes. Add diced egg whites to sauce. Spoon sauce over toast; top with crumbled egg yolks. Serves 2 to 4.

Hard-boiled eggs the easy way! Place eggs in a saucepan, add enough water to cover them by an inch and set over medium-high heat. As soon as the water comes to a boil, cover the pan and remove from heat. Let stand for 18 to 20 minutes. Then drain, cool in ice water and peel.

Granny Judy's Granola

Judy Borecky
Escondido, CA

After I sampled a fabulous granola at a restaurant in my area, I tried to copy the recipe at home. I think I came pretty close...it's delicious! The cranberries stay soft because they're added to the already-baked granola.

3 c. old-fashioned oats, uncooked
3 c. pecan halves
2 c. flaked coconut
14-oz. fat-free sweetened condensed milk

1/2 c. regular or reduced-calorie butter, melted
1/2 t. salt
1 c. sweetened dried cranberries

In a large bowl, combine all ingredients except cranberries; stir until blended. Spread on a 15"x10" jelly-roll pan that has been sprayed with non-stick vegetable spray. Bake at 250 degrees for 90 minutes, stirring after one hour. Remove from oven; add cranberries. Cool completely; store in an airtight container. Makes about 9 cups.

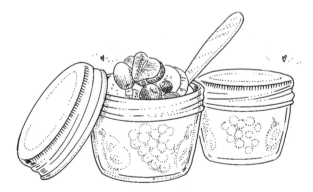

Half-pint Mason jars are just right for filling with layers of fresh fruit, creamy yogurt and crunchy granola. They can even be popped into the fridge the night before, then topped with cereal just before serving. Add a spoon and breakfast is served!

Wake up, *Sunshine!*

Chilled Fruit Compote

Claudia Keller
Carrollton, GA

Whenever we had breakfast at my grandmother's house, we could count on her to have a bowl of this scrumptious fruit salad ready to pull from the icebox. Sometimes she'd add a few maraschino cherries for color...we kids begged for those!

3/4 c. pineapple juice
2/3 c. orange juice
1 T. lemon juice
1/2 c. sugar
2 T. cornstarch
3 apples, cored and diced

2 bananas, sliced
20-oz. can pineapple chunks, drained
15-oz. can mandarin oranges, drained

In a saucepan over medium heat, mix fruit juices, sugar and cornstarch. Cook until thick and bubbly, stirring often. Remove from heat; set aside. Mix fruit pieces in a serving bowl. Pour the warm sauce over fruit; stir gently to coat. Cover and refrigerate for at least 3 hours. Serve chilled. Makes 8 servings.

Keep grocery shopping simple...make a shopping list that includes all the ingredients you use often, plus a few blank lines for special items.

Apple-Pecan French Toast

Leona Krivda Belle
Vernon, PA

*When my grandkids come to stay, I like to make something special,
just for them. I even sprinkle each plate with powdered sugar.*

1 loaf French bread, cut into
   12 slices, 1-inch thick
4 eggs, beaten
1 c. milk
1/4 c. sugar
1/4 t. cinnamon
1/2 t. vanilla extract

1 Jonathan or McIntosh apple,
   peeled, cored and shredded
1/2 c. chopped pecans
2 T. butter, melted
Garnish: maple syrup,
   fresh berries

Spray a 13"x9" glass baking pan with non-stick vegetable spray.
Arrange bread in a single layer in pan; set aside. In a large bowl, whisk
together eggs, milk, sugar, cinnamon, vanilla and apples. Pour egg
mixture over bread; turn bread over to coat each slice well. Cover with
plastic wrap and refrigerate overnight. In the morning, sprinkle with
pecans; drizzle with melted butter. Bake at 425 degrees for 20 to
25 minutes, until golden. Serve with maple syrup and fresh berries.
Serves 6, 2 slices each.

Grandma's Corn Cakes

Ruth Ann Evans
Franklin Furnace, OH

*This was my grandma's recipe and she would make them
silver-dollar size for us whenever we visited her. So simple
to make, but very good!*

1 c, buttermilk
1/2 t. baking soda
1 c. cornmeal

1/8 t. salt
1/2 c. all-purpose flour
butter for frying

Combine all ingredients in a bowl; whisk well. Drop batter by
tablespoonfuls or 1/4 cupfuls onto a buttered griddle over medium
heat. Cook until golden on bottom; turn over and cook until other
side is done. Makes 6 servings.

Wake up, *Sunshine!*

Nana's Wedge Pancakes

Patricia O'Kins Johnson
Snoqualmie, WA

Years ago, my mother came up with this unique way of preparing pancakes so she could serve both of her grandkids at the same time. The kids ask for it every time we visit!

2/3 c. all-purpose flour
2/3 c. whole-wheat flour
2/3 c. quick-cooking oats, uncooked
6 T. sugar, divided
4 t. baking powder

1/2 t. salt
2 eggs, beaten
2-1/3 c. milk
1/4 c. oil
1-1/2 t. cinnamon
3 to 4 T. butter, softened

In a bowl, combine flours, oats, 2 tablespoons sugar, baking powder and salt; set aside. In a large bowl, whisk together eggs, milk and oil. Add flour mixture to egg mixture; mix well. Batter will be thin. Let batter stand for 5 minutes. Combine cinnamon and remaining sugar in a cup. Lightly grease a griddle; heat until a water droplet sizzles on the surface. Pour 1/2 cup batter onto griddle; spread to 7 or 8 inches in diameter. Cook until fairly dry on top. Turn and cook other side until lightly golden. When pancake is done, remove to a plate. Spread generously with a teaspoon of butter; evenly sprinkle with a teaspoon of cinnamon-sugar. Continue with remaining ingredients. As more pancakes are done, stack on top of previously cooked pancakes to make 8 layers. To serve, cut into wedges like a pie. Serves 4.

Keep a tin of apple pie spice on hand to jazz up pancakes, muffins and coffee cakes. A quick shake adds cinnamon, nutmeg and allspice all at once.

19

Granny's Biscuits & Milk Gravy

Tina Goodpasture
Meadowview, VA

I can still see my granny fixing breakfast every morning. Fried apples, gravy and bread, sausage, bacon and coffee...can you smell it? For a real treat, add some crumbled fried sausage to the gravy.

3 c. all-purpose flour
2 T. sugar
2-1/2 t. baking powder
1/2 t. baking soda

1/2 t. salt
1/2 c. shortening
1 c. buttermilk
1/4 c. butter, melted and divided

In a bowl, combine flour, sugar, baking powder, baking soda and salt. Cut in shortening with a fork or with your hands until mixture resembles cornmeal. Add buttermilk, a little at a time, stirring constantly until well mixed. Turn dough out onto a lightly floured surface; knead lightly 2 to 3 times. Roll out dough with a floured rolling pin to 1/2-inch thickness. Cut with a 2" biscuit cutter. Place biscuits in a greased cast-iron skillet. Gently press down top of biscuits. Brush biscuits with half of the melted butter. Bake at 450 degrees for 14 minutes, or until golden. Brush hot biscuits with remaining butter. To serve, split biscuits and ladle Milk Gravy over top. Serves 6.

Milk Gravy:

1/4 c. bacon drippings
1/4 c. all-purpose flour
1-1/2 c. milk, warmed

1/4 t. salt
1/4 t. pepper, or more to taste

Heat drippings in a cast-iron skillet over medium heat. Add flour; whisk until smooth and bubbly, about one minute. Add warm milk slowly and bring to a boil. Reduce heat to a low simmer. Cook and stir until thickened, about 5 minutes, adding more milk if necessary to desired thickness. Season with salt and pepper.

Don't have a biscuit cutter handy?
Use the end of a clean, empty soup
can to cut biscuit dough.

Granny Brown's Chocolate Gravy

Tia Beltz
Georgetown, KY

This chocolate gravy is smooth and rich, just like my great-grandmother's. The recipe has been handed down through four generations and so many warm and tender memories go with it. A plate of hot, made-from-scratch biscuits was always served with this family favorite!

2 c. milk	3 T. self-rising flour
3/4 c. sugar	1 t. vanilla extract
3 T. baking cocoa	

Heat milk in a large saucepan over medium-low heat until just warm. In a large bowl, mix sugar, cocoa and flour well; stir into warm milk. Bring to a boil for one minute, stirring constantly. Add vanilla; let stand until thickened. Serve warm. Makes 4 to 6 servings.

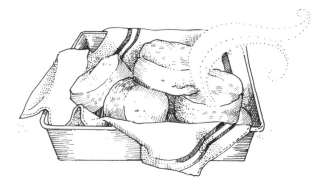

An old secret for the flakiest biscuits! Just stir to moisten and gently roll or pat the dough...don't overmix it.

Grandmother's Eggie in a Cup

Kate Carroll
Delaware, OH

*My grandmother used to make this for me. She always put it in
a special mug and it tasted so good. Enjoy your eggie in a cup!*

2 eggs
2 slices bread, toasted and diced

salt and pepper to taste

In a saucepan over medium-high heat, cover eggs with water. Boil for
20 minutes; immediately remove from heat. Peel eggs; they should be
a little less than hard-boiled. Put toast squares into one to 2 mugs.
Add eggs to toast; season with salt and pepper. Stir until toast is
coated with egg. Makes one to 2 servings.

Egg in a Nest

Jennie Gist
Gooseberry Patch

*Mom used to make this old favorite for us as kids, and then
for the grandkids. Dad always ate his with catsup!*

1 slice bread
2 t. butter, softened

1 egg
salt and pepper

Cut the center from bread with a cookie cutter. Spread butter on both
sides of bread. Place bread in a lightly buttered skillet over medium
heat; cook until lightly toasted on the bottom. Crack egg into the hole
in bread; season with salt and pepper. Cook until egg is partially set;
turn and cook to desired consistency. Serves one.

A home without a grandmother is like an egg without salt.

– Anonymous

Wake up, *Sunshine!*

Grandma's Fried Potatoes & Eggs

Jen Brooks
Jacksonville, IL

Growing up, this was my favorite meal that my grandma made! It's good for dinner as well as breakfast.

3 T. oil
8 potatoes, thinly sliced
1 onion, chopped
1 to 2 cloves garlic, minced

8 eggs, beaten
1 t. salt, or to taste
1 t. pepper, or to taste

In a large skillet over medium heat, combine oil, potatoes, onion and garlic. Cook until tender, about 10 minutes. Whisk eggs with salt and pepper. Add eggs to skillet; reduce heat to low and cook until scrambled. Makes 8 servings.

Easy Fried Apples

Judy Taylor
Butler, MO

I cannot perfect these apples to what my mother made, but this is my version. These apples are delicious with sausage for breakfast and with pork chops for dinner. There's no need to peel them.

1/3 c. margarine
3/4 c. brown sugar, packed

6 to 8 large Jonathan apples,
   cored and sliced

Melt margarine in a large skillet over medium heat. Add brown sugar; cook and stir until syrupy. Add apple slices and stir to coat. Cook until apples are soft and golden. Makes 4 servings.

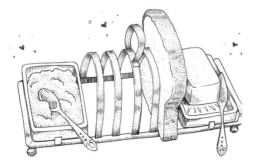

Serve up sweet memories. Bring out Grandma's vintage toast rack and jelly dish to use on the breakfast table.

Rhubarb Coffee Cake

Mary Muchowicz
Elk Grove Village, IL

My mother and my aunt both used to make this coffee cake. We never suspected it wasn't apple until they told us it was rhubarb. It is so delicious...a great way to use up rhubarb when you have a bumper crop.

1-1/2 c. sugar, divided
3/4 c. milk
1/4 c. butter, softened
1 egg, beaten
1 t. vanilla extract
1-3/4 c. all-purpose flour
1 t. baking soda

1/8 t. salt
2 c. rhubarb, finely chopped
1/2 c. brown sugar, packed
1 t. cinnamon
1/2 c. chopped nuts
Optional: whipped cream

In a large bowl, blend one cup sugar, milk, butter, egg and vanilla; set aside. In a separate bowl, mix flour, baking soda and salt. Add flour mixture to sugar mixture; stir well. Stir in rhubarb. Pour batter into a greased 12"x9" baking pan; set aside. In another bowl, mix together remaining sugar, brown sugar, cinnamon and nuts. Sprinkle mixture over batter. Bake at 350 degrees for 35 to 40 minutes. Serve warm, topped with whipped cream, if desired. Makes 15 servings.

Saturday morning is perfect for an old-fashioned kaffeeklatsch to chat over coffee cake and coffee. Invite a girlfriend, or the new neighbor you've been wanting to get to know better, to share the latest news...you'll be so glad you did!

Wake up, *Sunshine!*

Aunt Ella Mae's Raised Doughnuts

Patricia Parker
Cabool, MO

My daddy's sister Ella Mae was a wonderful cook. These doughnuts were one of her specialties. I miss her.

2 potatoes, peeled and quartered
2 envs. active dry yeast
1-1/2 c. warm water, 110 to
    115 degrees
1 c. sugar
1-1/4 t. salt

2 eggs, beaten
2/3 c. shortening
6-1/2 to 7 c. all-purpose flour
oil for frying
Garnish: sugar for coating

Cover potatoes with water in a saucepan. Cook over medium-high heat until tender, 10 to 15 minutes. Drain well; mash potatoes and measure out one cup. In a large bowl, dissolve yeast in warm water. Add mashed potatoes, sugar and salt; stir until mixed. Let stand about 20 minutes. Stir in eggs and shortening. Add flour, one cupful at a time, until a soft dough forms. Cover and let rise for one to 2 hours, until double in size. Roll out dough on a floured surface; cut out with a doughnut cutter. Let rise again until double in size. In a deep pan, heat several inches oil to about 375 degrees. Add doughnuts, a few at a time, and cook until golden on both sides. Remove with a slotted spoon; drain on paper towels. Sprinkle with sugar, if desired. Makes 4 dozen.

Vintage recipes always called for flour to be sifted. Nowadays, though, that isn't necessary for all-purpose flour. Just stir, spoon lightly into a measuring cup and level off.

Mother's Sticky Buns

Ruth Crumm
Springfield, MO

These are most delicious served warm, any time of the day!
My mother made sticky buns every Christmas Eve and served
them for breakfast with fresh fruit on Christmas morning.

1 T. active dry yeast
1-1/4 c. warm water, 110 to
   115 degrees
1/4 c. oil
1/4 c. sugar
1 egg, beaten

1 t. salt
3 to 4 c. all-purpose flour
1 c. butter, softened and divided
2 c. brown sugar, packed and
   divided
cinnamon to taste

In a large bowl, combine yeast, warm water, oil and sugar. Stir; let cool to lukewarm. Some bubbles will form on top. Add egg, salt and enough flour to form a soft dough. Cover and allow to rise for 2 hours in a warm place. Melt 1/2 cup butter; add to a 13"x9" baking pan. Add one cup brown sugar to melted butter; mix with a fork and set aside. This is the syrup the rolls will bake in. Punch down the risen dough; roll out on a floured surface into a rectangle, about 1/4-inch thick. Spread dough with remaining butter. Sprinkle remaining brown sugar over butter; sprinkle generously with cinnamon. Starting with one long side of rectangle, roll up tightly. Slice dough one-inch thick. Lay rolls cut-side up in the syrup. Cover and allow to rise until rolls rise to the top of the pan. Bake at 350 degrees for 30 minutes, or until golden; do not overbake. Remove from oven; place a rectangular serving tray or platter over the rolls. With protected hands, quickly flip pan upside-down onto the platter. This is best done over the sink in case the syrup drips. Serve warm. Makes 10 buns.

If the water added to yeast is too hot, it will kill the yeast.
Use this trick to test the temperature...sprinkle the heated
water on your forearm. If it doesn't feel either hot or cold,
the temperature is just right.

Wake up, *Sunshine!*

Italian Breakfast Cake

Cheryl Daley
Hazelton, PA

My grandmother made this scrumptious cake all the time
when I was a kid. The smell of warm oranges is wonderful!

1 c. sugar
3 T. shortening
1 T. butter, softened
3 eggs, beaten
1 c. milk

4 c. all-purpose flour
3 T. baking powder
1/8 t. salt
2 T. orange or vanilla extract
zest and juice of 1 orange

In a large bowl, mix together all ingredients until a sticky dough
forms. Pat dough into a greased and floured 13"x9" baking pan.
Bake at 350 degrees for 60 minutes, or until cake tests done with a
toothpick. Serves 12.

Sweet Oranges

Jill Ball
Highland, UT

I love fruit for breakfast, lunch, dinner and anytime in between.
This is a different way to fix oranges...yummy and easy.

4 navel oranges, peeled and
   cut into segments
2 T. orange juice

2 T. lemon juice
1 T. sugar
1/4 t. cinnamon

Arrange orange segments on a plate; set aside. In a cup, whisk
together fruit juices. Add sugar and cinnamon; mix well. Spoon
mixture over oranges and serve immediately. Serves 4.

Save that orange half after it's been
juiced! Wrap it and store in the
freezer, ready to grate whenever a
recipe calls for fresh citrus zest.

Brown Sugar-Blueberry Muffins *Karen Van Den Berge*
Holland, MI

An old recipe from my mom, who loved surprising us with these warm muffins for breakfast. I've made them numerous times for coffee with friends. Every time, they say, "These are the best blueberry muffins I've ever tasted!"

2 c. blueberries, thawed if frozen	3 eggs, beaten
3 c. all-purpose flour, divided	1 t. baking soda
1 c. margarine, softened	1/2 t. salt
2 c. brown sugar, packed	1 c. milk

Roll blueberries in 1/2 cup flour; set aside. In a large bowl, blend together margarine, brown sugar and eggs. In another bowl, mix remaining flour and baking soda; mix well. Add to margarine mixture along with milk; stir until moistened. Fold in blueberries. Fill greased muffin cups 2/3 full. Bake at 375 degrees for 25 minutes. Makes 2 dozen.

Quilter's Coffee

Tina Goodpasture
Meadowview, VA

My granny always made quilts from scraps...she never wasted anything. The last one she made was called an "H" quilt, because our family name was Hudson. I still have that quilt!

4 c. freshly brewed coffee	1 t. cinnamon
3 c. warm milk	1/2 t. ground ginger

Combine all ingredients in a large saucepan; whisk together. Heat over medium-low heat until hot. Serve immediately. Makes 8 servings.

Most muffin batters can be stirred up the night before and can even be scooped into muffin cups ahead of time. Simply cover and refrigerate. In the morning, pop them in the oven.

Wake up, *Sunshine!*

Cherry Kuchen

Kathy Benkow
East Aurora, NY

This is my grandmother's recipe, and it was one of my favorite breakfast treats when I was growing up. OK, so it still is! It's so easy, sweet, and delicious.

1 c. margarine	1 t. baking powder
1 c. sugar	1 t. vanilla extract
2 eggs, beaten	21-oz. can cherry pie filling
2 c. all-purpose flour	

In a bowl, blend margarine, sugar and eggs. Add flour, baking powder and vanilla; mix well. Spread 2/3 of batter in a greased 13"x9" baking pan. Spoon pie filling on top. Dollop remaining batter over pie filling by large spoonfuls. Bake at 350 degrees for 40 minutes, until golden. Makes 15 servings.

Vintage rotary mixers can be found at flea markets and tag sales. They're handy for mixing up batters and scrambling eggs quickly and easily.

Family Breakfast Feast

Mandy Hardy
Middleville, MI

My grandmother used to make a version of this during cold winter months when we had family gatherings. It is a hearty and easy bake-up for a hungry crew.

32-oz. pkg. frozen shredded
   hashbrowns
16-oz. container sour cream
10-3/4 oz. can Cheddar cheese
   soup
4-oz. can mushroom pieces,
   drained
10-3/4 oz. can cream of
   mushroom soup

14-oz. pkg. mini smoked
   sausages, sliced
1 t. onion salt
1 t. salt
1 t. pepper
1/2 c. onion, chopped
8-oz. pkg. shredded Cheddar
   cheese, divided
2.8-oz. can French fried onions

In a greased 13"x9" glass baking pan, layer frozen hashbrowns, sour cream, cheese soup, mushrooms, mushroom soup and sausages. Sprinkle with seasonings. Stir gently; spread out in pan. Cover with chopped onion and half of shredded cheese. Bake, uncovered, at 375 degrees for 45 minutes. Stir; top with desired amount of French fried onions and sprinkle with remaining cheese. Bake for 20 more minutes. Cool slightly before serving. Serves 8.

Serve tender poached eggs with breakfast potatoes or hash. Fill a skillet with water. Add a dash of vinegar and heat until simmering. Swirl the water with a spoon and gently slide in an egg from a saucer. Let cook until set, 3 to 4 minutes, and remove the egg with a slotted spoon.

Hot Soup
to Warm You Up!

Fresh Tomato Soup

Joyce Penn
Columbus, OH

*A favorite of my mother's...tomatoes fresh from the garden,
into the soup pot. Yum!*

1 to 2 T. olive or canola oil
1 c. yellow onion, coarsely
   chopped
1 red pepper, coarsely chopped
2 T. onion soup mix
1 T. garlic, minced

6 tomatoes or 10 roma tomatoes,
   coarsely chopped
3/4 t. salt, or to taste
1/2 t. pepper, or to taste
Optional: chopped fresh chives

Heat oil in a large saucepan over medium-low heat; add onion, red pepper, soup mix and garlic. Cook for 5 minutes, until onion is translucent. Stir in tomatoes, salt and pepper. Bring to a boil; reduce heat to low. Cover and simmer, stirring occasionally, for 20 minutes or until tomatoes are very soft. Remove from heat. When cool enough to handle, transfer mixture in batches to a blender or food processor; process until soupy but still slightly chunky. May reheat and serve hot, serve at room temperature or chill before serving. Sprinkle with chives, if desired. Serves 4.

Nothing perks up the flavor of tomato soup like fresh basil!
Keep a pot of basil in the kitchen windowsill and just pinch off
a few leaves whenever they're needed.

Colby Corn Chowder

Vickie
Gooseberry Patch

You'll love this creamy, hearty chowder! Crumbled bacon makes a delicious garnish, so cook up a few extra slices. If Colby cheese isn't available, mild Cheddar will be delicious too.

6 potatoes, peeled and diced
1 t. salt
1 onion, chopped
1/4 c. butter
2 14-3/4 oz. cans creamed corn

4 slices bacon, cooked and
    crisply crumbled
3 c. milk
8-oz. pkg. Colby cheese, cubed

Place potatoes in a soup pot; sprinkle with salt and cover with water. Bring to a boil over medium heat. Cover and simmer until potatoes are tender. Meanwhile, in a skillet over medium heat, sauté onion in butter until tender. Stir in corn and bacon; heat through. Drain potatoes; return to pot. Add milk and heat through over low heat. Stir in corn mixture and cheese; stir until cheese is melted. Serve immediately. Makes 12 to 14 servings.

Oops! If soup starts to burn on the bottom, all is not lost. Spoon it into another pan, being careful not to scrape up the scorched part on the bottom. The burnt taste usually won't linger. To avoid burnt soup the next time, cook over low heat and stir often.

California Avocado Soup

Charlotte Orm
Florence, AZ

My grandmother used to grow her own avocados, and she always used some of them to make this delicious soup. Grandma passed away several years ago, and I wanted to share this recipe with other avocado lovers.

1/2 c. onion, chopped
1 T. butter
2 14-1/2 oz. cans chicken broth
2 potatoes, peeled and cubed
1/2 t. salt

1/4 t. pepper
2 ripe avocados, halved
   and pitted
1/2 c. sour cream
1/4 c. real bacon bits

In a large saucepan over medium heat, sauté onion in butter until tender. Add broth, potatoes, salt and pepper; bring to a boil. Reduce heat to low. Cover and simmer for 15 to 25 minutes, until potatoes are tender. Remove from heat; cool slightly. Working in batches, scoop avocado pulp into a blender; add potato mixture with broth. Cover and process until puréed. Return to pan; heat through. Garnish with sour cream and bacon bits. Serves 6.

Vegetable Beef Soup

Janet Maynard
Perry, FL

On cold nights, this soup will warm you up. It's been handed down from grandmother to mother to daughter...still a family favorite.

5 lbs. potatoes, peeled and cubed
3 lbs. stew beef cubes
28-oz. can whole tomatoes

10-oz. pkg. frozen mixed
   vegetables
salt and pepper to taste

To a 6-quart slow cooker, add potatoes and beef. Mash tomatoes with juice and add along with remaining ingredients. Cover and cook on low setting for 7 to 8 hours. Makes 10 to 12 servings.

Hot Soup
to Warm You Up!

Caboosta Cabbage Soup

Janae Mallonee
Marlboro, MA

I am part Italian and part Lithuanian...this means I pretty much live on bread, pasta and potato. No low-carb diet in my future! It's my mother's side that is Lithuanian, and we eat a lot of really good Polish food. This soup recipe has been passed down from generation to generation. It's not fancy, it's just comforting and delicious! It's so simple to make, even after years of making it, I still feel like I am forgetting something!

6 c. water
28-oz. can crushed tomatoes
1/2 to 2/3 head cabbage,
   shredded

1-1/2 c. cooked pork, diced
1 bay leaf
salt and pepper to taste

In a soup pot over medium heat, combine water, tomatoes with juice, cabbage, pork and bay leaf. Bring to a boil; reduce heat to low. Simmer for about 30 minutes, stirring occasionally, until pork is cooked and cabbage is tender. At serving time, discard bay leaf; season with salt and pepper. Makes 8 servings.

As any grandmother can tell you, homemade soup always tastes better the next day! After being refrigerated overnight, it's a snap to skim off the fat too.

Creamy Chicken & Gnocchi Soup

Annie Keplar
California, PA

The ultimate comfort food...especially when Gram makes it.
Cornstarch gives it a chowder consistency, but if you prefer
a thinner soup, just use a little less cornstarch.

1/2 onion, diced
1 stalk celery, diced
1/2 carrot, peeled and shredded
1 clove garlic, diced
1 T. olive oil
3 boneless, skinless chicken
    breasts, cooked and diced
4 c. chicken broth
2 c. half-and-half

1 T. dried thyme
1/8 t. salt
1/8 t. pepper
16-oz. pkg. gnocchi pasta,
    uncooked
1/2 c. fresh spinach, chopped
1 T. cornstarch
2 T. cold water

In a large soup pot over medium heat, sauté onion, celery, carrot and garlic in oil until onion is translucent. Stir in chicken, chicken broth, half-and-half and seasonings; bring to a boil. Add gnocchi; cook for 4 minutes. Reduce heat to medium-low. Continue cooking for 10 minutes, stirring often. Add spinach; cook for one to 2 minutes, until spinach is wilted. In a cup, dissolve cornstarch in cold water. Return soup to boiling; add cornstarch mixture. Cook and stir until thickened. Serves 4.

A soup secret! The rind from fresh Parmesan cheese gives soup rich flavor. Toss the rind into the soup just as it begins to simmer. When soup is done, any undissolved pieces can be spooned out.

Beef Barley Soup

Pieterina Hengstmengel
Alberta, Canada

This recipe is my mom's and many people have requested it. Sometimes she adds catsup to enhance the color, and it's delicious either way. It's quick & easy...so perfect for a cold winter's day!

1 lb. ground beef
1 onion, chopped
1/2 c. celery, chopped
2 t. Worcestershire sauce
1 t. dried basil
3 c. water
1 c. quick-cooking barley, uncooked
1 T. butter
1 t. salt
2 14-1/2 oz. cans beef broth
2 14-1/2 oz. cans diced tomatoes
Optional: 1/4 c. catsup

In a skillet over medium heat, cook beef, onion and celery until beef is no longer pink and vegetables are tender. Drain; add Worcestershire sauce and basil. Meanwhile, in a soup pot over medium-high heat, bring water, barley, butter and salt to a boil. Reduce heat to medium-low. Cover and simmer for 10 to 20 minutes, until barley is tender. Stir in beef mixture, beef broth, tomatoes with juice and catsup, if using. Heat through over low heat, stirring occasionally. Makes 8 servings.

A large cast-iron Dutch oven is perfect for soups & stews.
It can handle the high heat desirable for browning ingredients
well, then conducts lower heat evenly for a good simmer.
It's versatile too...use for casseroles that start on the
stovetop, then are finished in the oven.

Casserole Onion Bread

Nancy Wise
Little Rock, AR

I don't know where Gram got this recipe, but she would
bake up a couple of loaves whenever she had soup simmering
on the stove. The kitchen always smelled so inviting!

2 envs. active dry yeast
1/2 c. warm water,
   110 to 115 degrees
3/4 c. milk
1/2 c. sugar

1/2 c. butter, sliced
1.35-oz. pkg. onion soup mix
1 egg, beaten
4 c. all-purpose flour, divided
Garnish: melted butter

In a cup, sprinkle yeast over warm water; stir to dissolve and set aside. In a small saucepan, heat milk over medium-low heat, stirring constantly, until almost boiling. Remove from heat. Add sugar and butter; stir until sugar dissolves and butter melts. In a large bowl, combine yeast mixture, warm milk mixture, soup mix, egg and 2 cups flour. Beat until smooth, about 2 minutes. Stir in remaining flour until a stiff dough forms. Cover tightly; chill at least 2 hours. Divide dough in half; flatten and press evenly into 2 greased 1-1/2 quart casserole dishes. Brush tops with melted butter; cover with tea towels. Let rise in a warm place until double. Bake at 375 degrees for about 35 minutes, until loaves sound hollow when tapped. Turn loaves out; brush with butter. Makes 2 loaves.

Here's how to tell when rising dough has doubled. Press 2 fingertips 1/2-inch deep into the dough, and then release. If the dent remains, the dough has doubled.

Mom's Zucchini Bread

Jamie Tomkins
Lakeside, AZ

My mom has made this bread for years and when I finally moved out, she gave me the recipe to make for my own family. It's great to bake something yummy that has some health benefits too...especially for a kid who doesn't know there's zucchini inside. Shh!

3 eggs	1 t. baking powder
1 c. oil	1 t. baking soda
2 c. sugar	1 t. salt
2 c. zucchini, grated	1 t. cinnamon
2 t. vanilla extract	1/2 c. chopped nuts
3 c. all-purpose flour	

Beat eggs in a bowl. Add oil, sugar, zucchini and vanilla; blend together. In a separate bowl, mix remaining ingredients except nuts. Add to egg mixture; stir well. Fold in nuts. Divide batter between 2 greased 9"x5" loaf pans, filling 1/2 to 3/4 full. Bake at 325 degrees for one hour, or until a toothpick inserted in the center comes out clean. Turn out loaves onto a wire rack to cool. Makes 2 loaves.

If raisins become dry or sugary, or if a recipe calls for "plumped" raisins, simply place the raisins in a bowl and cover with boiling water. Soak the raisins for 15 minutes, drain and pat dry using a paper towel.

Summer Vegetable Soup

Beth Stanton
Port Charlotte, FL

When I was younger, we lived in Arkansas. My mom planted a huge vegetable garden, so this soup was made often during summer months. It has just about every veggie you could think of in it! Complete the meal with toasted garlic bread or Caesar salad.

2 T. olive oil
1 c. leek, white and green parts,
   thinly sliced
1/2 c. carrot, peeled and grated
2 to 3 cloves garlic, minced
1 t. fresh oregano
4 c. chicken broth
14-1/2 oz. can diced tomatoes
15-1/2 oz. can Great Northern
   beans, drained, rinsed and
   divided

1 c. summer squash, chopped
1 c. zucchini, chopped
1/2 c. fresh or frozen corn
1/2 c. ditalini pasta, uncooked
1/2 t. kosher salt
1/2 t. pepper
2 c. fresh baby spinach
Garnish: basil pesto sauce,
   shredded Asiago cheese

Heat oil in a large Dutch oven over medium heat. Add leek, carrot, garlic and oregano. Cover and cook for 5 minutes, stirring occasionally. Add chicken broth and tomatoes with juice; bring to a boil. Reduce heat to low; simmer for 15 minutes. Place half of the beans in a bowl; mash with a fork. Add mashed beans, remaining beans, squash, zucchini, corn, uncooked pasta, salt and pepper to Dutch oven. Increase heat to medium; simmer for 10 minutes. Stir in spinach and cook for 3 more minutes, until wilted. To serve, ladle soup into bowls. Top each serving with a teaspoon of pesto and a tablespoon of cheese. Serves 4.

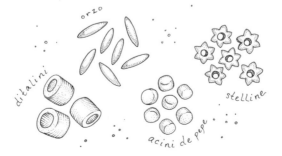

Tiny pasta shapes like ditalini, orzo, acini di pepe and stelline or stars are all quick-cooking and ideal for soup, so choose your favorite.

Cream of Asparagus Soup

Alice Livermore
Rochester, NY

I'm a grandmother with grandkids from 12 to 22 and we all love to eat. I grew up in Kansas where we grew big gardens and big eaters. While picking fresh asparagus, the owner of the patch gave me her more-or-less recipe and I've adapted it to my version. It makes a wonderful meal starter. Everyone loves it at our house, including the grandkids.

4 c. chicken broth
pepper to taste
1 to 1-1/2 lbs. fresh asparagus,
   trimmed and broken into
    1-inch pieces
1 onion, chopped

1/4 c. butter, sliced
4 c. half-and-half and/or milk
8-oz. pkg. American cheese,
   diced, or shredded Cheddar
   cheese
Optional: celery seed to taste

In a soup pot, bring chicken broth and pepper to a boil. Add asparagus and onion; reduce heat to medium-low. Cover and simmer until asparagus is very tender and falling apart. Add butter; stir until melted. Working in batches, process broth mixture in a blender. If a smoother texture is desired, strain broth mixture through a colander into another soup pot; press asparagus pulp through the colander. Return mixture to soup pot. Add half-and-half or milk, cheese and celery seed, if using. Cook and stir over medium-low heat until cheese is melted. Soup keeps well for several days in the refrigerator. Makes 6 to 8 servings.

Save celery leaves to add flavor to soups. Spread fresh celery leaves on a baking sheet and bake at 180 degrees for about 3 hours. When they're crisp, store them in a canning jar. To use, crumble the leaves into the soup pot.

Chicken Soup & Homemade Egg Noodles

Anita Gibson
Woodbury, MN

My mother used to make this recipe when I was growing up. My dad's family made this over his childhood as well. I have modified it a little over the years and my family loves it. Not many people make homemade noodles anymore so company loves it too. Served with hot buttered rolls, it's a wonderful lunch or supper.

5 to 6-lb. stewing chicken
6 c. chicken broth
4 carrots, peeled and diced
4 stalks celery, diced
1 T. fresh rosemary

16-oz. pkg. frozen mixed stew
 or soup vegetables
salt and pepper to taste
Optional: 1 t. lemon pepper

Place chicken in a large soup pot; add chicken broth, carrots, celery and rosemary. Bring to a boil over high heat; reduce heat to medium-low. Cover and simmer until chicken is tender, about 45 minutes. Remove chicken to a platter and let cool, reserving broth in pot. Chop chicken; return to broth. Return to a boil; reduce heat to low. Add frozen vegetables and seasonings. Simmer for one to 2 hours. Drop Egg Noodles into boiling soup; simmer for 30 minutes. Soup may be divided into several containers and frozen. Serves 8 to 10.

Egg Noodles:

2 eggs, beaten
1/4 c. milk

1 t. salt
2 c. all-purpose flour

In a bowl, stir together eggs, milk and salt. Stir in enough flour to make a stiff, sticky dough. Gather dough into a ball. Roll out very thinly on a floured surface; let stand for 20 minutes. Roll up dough loosely; slice 1/4-inch thick. Let stand until ready to add to soup, or leave out to dry overnight. May store dried noodles in a container.

In my grandmother's house there was always chicken soup
And talk of the old country...
– Louis Simpson

Grandma's Creamy Potato Soup

Carol Wengyn
Valrico, FL

I remember my sweet adorable grandmother peeling potatoes at the kitchen table. She would spread out newspaper to catch the peels and peel the potatoes as she watched her favorite game shows on TV.

5 potatoes, peeled and cut into
    bite-size cubes
12-oz. can evaporated milk
1-1/2 c. whole milk
1-1/2 c. water
1/2 c. butter, sliced

1 onion, quartered
1 stalk celery, chopped
garlic juice or powder to taste
1 t. salt
1/2 t. pepper

Place potatoes in a stockpot; add milks and water. Bring to a simmer over medium heat. Add butter; allow to melt. Add remaining ingredients; stir until well blended. Reduce heat to low; do not allow soup to boil. Simmer until potatoes are soft. Serves 4.

Kids are sure to know the old tale of Stone Soup...why not let it inspire a chilly-weather get-together? Invite everyone to bring a favorite veggie, while you provide a bubbling stockpot of broth. While the soup simmers, you can play board games or just chat for an old-fashioned good time.

Down-Home Soup Beans

Claire Bertram
Lexington, KY

An old-time comfort food! Granny always served this topped with chopped fresh onion and buttered cornbread on the side. Replace some of the water with chicken broth, if you like.

1 lb. dried Great Northern or
   pinto beans
12 c. water
1 to 1-1/2 c. cooked ham, diced
1 onion, diced
1 clove garlic, minced

1/4 t. red pepper flakes
1/2 t. salt
1 t. pepper
Optional: 1 c. baby carrots,
   sliced

Combine all ingredients in a large Dutch oven; bring to a boil. Reduce heat and simmer, stirring occasionally, until beans are very tender and beginning to pop, 1-1/2 to 2 hours. Add a little more water while simmering, as needed to make sure beans are just covered. Remove from heat. Transfer 2 cups of beans to a bowl and coarsely mash with a fork. Return mashed beans to pot; stir to combine and heat through. Serves 8.

Mom-Mom's Cornbread

Linda Payne
Snow Hill, MD

This is the cornbread my grandmother always made. Now I make a pan of her cornbread for every family function, to bring her memories back to the meal!

3 c. water
1/2 c. butter, sliced
1 c. sugar

2 c. cornmeal
2 eggs, beaten
1-1/2 c. milk

In a heavy saucepan over medium heat, combine water, butter and sugar. Bring to a boil. In a bowl, combine cornmeal, eggs and milk; mix well and add to boiling water mixture. Cook, stirring well, until thickened. Pour batter into a greased 8"x8" baking pan. Bake at 375 degrees for 45 to 60 minutes. Cut into squares; serve warm. Makes 9 servings.

Navy Bean Soup

Sandy Coffey
Cincinnati, OH

Best bean soup ever! This was even my favorite as a kid.
Long simmering allows all the flavors to blend together.

2 c. dried navy beans
1 meaty ham bone
12 c. water
1/2 c. mashed potatoes
1 to 1-1/2 c. onions,
   finely chopped

1/2 to 1 bunch celery, stalks
   and tops, chopped
1 clove garlic, minced
1/4 c. fresh parsley, finely
   chopped

Cover beans with water and soak overnight; drain. Put soaked beans, ham bone and 12 cups water in a soup kettle. Bring to a boil over medium heat; reduce heat to low. Cover and simmer for 2 hours, stirring occasionally. After 2 hours, stir in remaining ingredients. Simmer one more hour. Remove ham bone; dice meat and return to soup. Stir and serve. Makes 8 servings.

Dried beans are nutritious, inexpensive and come in lots
of varieties...perfect for delicious family meals. Before cooking,
place beans in a colander, rinse well and pick through,
discarding any small twigs or bits of debris.

Apple-Walnut Bread

Gloria Simmons
Greenville, MI

This recipe was handed down to me by my grandmother. I have wonderful childhood memories of learning how to bake with her.

2 c. sugar
1 c. oil
3 eggs, beaten
3 c. all-purpose flour
1 t. baking soda
1 t. salt

1 t. cinnamon
2 t. vanilla extract
3 c. cooking apples, peeled, cored and finely diced
1 c. chopped walnuts
Garnish: additional sugar

In a large bowl, beat together sugar, oil and eggs. In a separate bowl, mix flour, baking soda, salt and cinnamon; add to sugar mixture and stir well. Add vanilla; fold in apples and nuts. Divide batter evenly between 2 lightly greased and floured 9"x5" loaf pans. Sprinkle tops with sugar. Bake at 325 degrees for one hour, or until a toothpick inserted comes out clean. Makes 2 loaves.

Peanut Butter Bread

Patty Flak
Erie, PA

A treasure I found going through my Mimi's recipe box. I remember this bread so well...mmm!

1-3/4 c. all-purpose flour
1/2 c. sugar
2-1/2 t. baking powder
1/2 t. salt

1/2 c. creamy peanut butter
2 eggs, beaten
3/4 c. milk

In a bowl, mix together flour, sugar, baking powder and salt. Stir in peanut butter until mixture is crumbly. Add eggs and milk; stir until well combined. Turn into a well greased 9"x5" loaf pan. Bake at 350 degrees for about 45 minutes. Remove loaf from pan; cool on a wire rack. Makes one loaf.

Fresh-baked bread freezes beautifully. Cool and wrap it in plastic, then aluminum foil and freeze up to 3 weeks.

Hot Soup
to Warm You Up!

Grandma Bel's Honey Muffins

Dusty Allderdice
Loma, MT

Living in the country, my grandma always came up with recipes that could be made with a few ingredients that she had on hand. These muffins were a favorite for me as a child and now a favorite for my own kids. They're delicious anytime!

2 c. all-purpose flour	1 egg, beaten
1/2 c. sugar	1 c. milk
1 T. baking powder	1/4 c. butter, melted
1/2 t. salt	1/4 c. honey

Combine flour, sugar, baking powder and salt; set aside. In a separate large bowl, whisk egg, milk, butter and honey. Stir in flour mixture just until moistened. Fill 12 greased or paper-lined muffin cups 3/4 full. Bake at 350 degrees for 15 to 18 minutes, until a toothpick comes out clean. Serve warm. Makes one dozen.

Quick & Easy Biscuit Rolls

Kim Hartless
Forest, VA

This was my grandmother's go-to recipe whenever she didn't feel like making a full pan of biscuits. My grandfather expected fresh bread with every meal, so this was a fast option for her.

1 c. self-rising flour	2 T. mayonnaise
1/2 c. milk	

Add flour and milk to a bowl; stir well. Add mayonnaise; stir until mixed. Spoon batter into 6 greased muffin cups, filling 1/2 full. Bake at 400 degrees for 10 to 12 minutes, until golden. Recipe may be doubled for a 12-cup muffin tin. Makes 6 rolls.

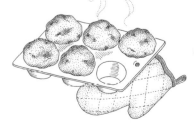

If a muffin recipe doesn't fill all the cups in your muffin tin, fill the empty cups with water. The muffins will bake more evenly.

Beginner's Chili

Denise Evans
Moosic, PA

My mother-in-law gave me this recipe when my husband and I were first married. I had never made chili before...since then, this is the only chili I eat! Twenty years later, I still make my chili using this recipe. Maybe it can help a new bride make her family happy too. You get a little sweetness and just a little hotness, but not so much kids can't eat it. A little secret: the ground beef must be mashed really fine as you're frying. It gives that special texture that's so good!

1 lb. ground beef
1 onion, diced
1/2 green pepper, diced
1 clove garlic, diced
2 10-3/4 oz. cans tomato soup
6-oz. can tomato paste
3-1/4 c. water
1/2 t. chili powder
1/8 t. red pepper flakes

Optional: 1/8 t. cayenne pepper
1/8 t. dried oregano
1/8 t. salt
1/8 t. pepper
1 bay leaf
16-oz. kidney beans
cooked rice and/or cornbread
Optional: sour cream, shredded
   Cheddar cheese

In a Dutch oven over medium heat, brown beef with onion, green pepper and garlic. Mash beef with a wooden spatula as finely as possible. Drain; stir in tomato soup, tomato paste, water and seasonings. Reduce heat to low. Cover and simmer for one hour, stirring occasionally. Lightly mash kidney beans with a fork in a bowl; stir into chili. Cook another 10 minutes. Discard bay leaf. Serve chili ladled over cooked rice or cornbread, or serve cornbread on the side. Top with a dollop of sour cream and a handful of cheese, if you wish. Serves 4 to 6.

If your pot of chili turned out too spicy, tame the heat by stirring in a spoonful of honey.

Hot Soup
to Warm You Up!

Bess's Taco Soup

Dawnda Willibey
Tulsa, OK

This simple recipe came from my mother. It's a good standby warm-you-up soup. Serve with shredded cheese and tortilla chips...delicious!

1 lb. ground beef
1/2 c. onion, chopped
3 14-1/2 oz. cans stewed
   tomatoes
10-oz. can diced tomatoes &
   green chiles
16-oz. can pinto beans &
   jalapeño peppers

16-oz. can pinto beans
16-oz. can kidney beans
15-1/2 oz. can hominy
1-1/4 oz. pkg. taco seasoning
   mix
1-oz. pkg. ranch salad dressing
   mix
1 to 2 c. water

In a soup pot over medium heat, cook beef with onion until browned; drain. Add tomatoes with juice, beans, hominy and seasoning mixes. Add water to desired consistency. Stir until blended. Reduce heat to medium-low; simmer for 30 minutes, stirring occasionally. Makes 6 to 8 servings.

Grandma was a champ at stretching a pot of soup to feed a few extra guests. Some easy add-ins are canned beans, canned tomatoes and cooked orzo pasta. Simmer for just a few minutes, until heated through.

Black-Eyed Pea Soup

Dayna Jackson
Maricopa, AZ

Whenever I make this soup, I think of my grandma. Grandma always used to give each of us two cans of black-eyed peas at Christmas, to serve on New Year's Day for a new year of prosperity. Some relatives would give me their cans because they didn't care for them. I tried many recipes and finally came up with my own. Sometimes I make chili-cheese cornbread to go with it.

5 slices bacon
1/2 c. onion, finely diced
2 15-oz. cans black-eyed peas
10-oz. can diced tomatoes & green chiles
14-oz. can beef broth

salt and pepper to taste
1/2 c. shredded sharp Cheddar cheese
Garnish: tortilla or corn chips, additional shredded Cheddar cheese

In a skillet over medium heat, cook bacon until lightly crisp. Remove bacon from pan; crumble and set aside. Sauté onion in bacon drippings until tender; drain. In a large saucepan, stir together crumbled bacon, onion, peas with juice, tomatoes with juice, beef broth, salt and pepper. Cook over medium-high heat until nearly boiling; reduce heat to low. Simmer for 20 minutes. Stir in cheese. Continue to simmer over low heat for another 20 minutes. To serve, put a handful of chips in each bowl, ladle soup over chips and sprinkle with cheese. Serves 4.

Save bacon drippings in a jar in the fridge. Add just a little to the oil when frying potatoes or cooking green beans for delicious country-style flavor.

Aunties' Hot Dog Soup

Janae Mallonee
Marlboro, MA

This soup has been made by all of my aunties. I know, it's not the most appealing name ever, but it is what it is! My husband argued with me on this for years. One day he actually tasted it...and now he asks for it specifically! Such a comfort food, a big bowl of this soup on a cold New England night!

3 potatoes, peeled and diced
3 onions, sliced
1 c. baby carrots, sliced
23-oz. can cream of mushroom
   soup

2-1/2 c. milk
3 to 5 hot dogs, sliced
seasoned salt and pepper
   to taste

Combine potatoes, onions and carrots in a large saucepan; cover with water. Cook over medium-high heat until nearly tender; drain.Whisk together soup and milk; stir in hot dogs. Cook over medium-low heat until warmed through. Season to taste with salt and pepper. Makes 4 to 6 servings.

Soup suppers are a fuss-free way to get together with friends, neighbors and family. Each family brings a favorite soup to share, along with the recipe. What a delicious way to try a variety of soups!

Grandma's Chicken Noodle Soup

Laura Wirsig
Colorado Springs, CO

*This old-fashioned chicken noodle soup has a surprise ingredient...
a pinch of nutmeg that adds depth to the flavor. I adapted it from a
basic recipe and my family raves over it. My children don't like
carrots in their noodle soup, but (shhh) they don't even know the
finely grated carrots are in there!*

1 T. butter
1/4 c. onion, minced
1/4 t. celery salt
8 c. chicken broth
1-1/2 c. cooked chicken
    breast, diced
1/2 c. carrot, peeled and
    finely grated

1/2 t. dried oregano
1/2 t. dried basil
1/4 t. nutmeg
1-1/2 c. fine egg noodles,
    uncooked, or more
    to taste

Melt butter in a large pot over medium heat; add onion and celery
salt. Sauté until tender, about 3 to 5 minutes. Add remaining
ingredients; bring to a boil. Reduce heat to medium-low. Simmer for
about 20 minutes, stirring occasionally, until noodles are cooked.
Makes 8 servings.

Chicken backs and wings are excellent for making rich, delicious
broth...a terrific way to use up the last of farm-raised fowl. Save up
unused ones in the freezer until you have enough for a pot of broth.

Beefy Hamburger Soup

Chris Gravanda
Alden, NY

This recipe has been in our family for years. It's so chunky and delicious, especially with crusty bread. I remember when my grandmother used to make it for us as kids, and when I became a mother of three, I made it for my family. Today, my children are adults and make it for their own families.

1 lb. ground beef
14-1/2 oz. can whole tomatoes,
   cut up
8-oz. can tomato sauce
6-oz. can tomato paste
1 c. onion, chopped
1 c. celery, chopped
1 c. carrots, peeled and sliced

1/3 c. pearled barley, uncooked
1/4 c. catsup
1 T. beef bouillon granules
2 t. seasoned salt
1 t. dried basil
salt and pepper to taste
1 bay leaf

In a large saucepan over medium heat, brown beef, stirring lightly to break up any large pieces. Drain; add tomatoes with juice and remaining ingredients; bring to a boil. Reduce heat to low. Cover and simmer for one hour, stirring occasionally. Remove bay leaf before serving. Makes 6 to 8 servings.

Bay leaves are a must in many soup recipes, but it's best to remove before serving the soup. Tuck them into a metal tea ball that can hang on the side of the soup pot...easy to remove when done.

Grandma's Tomato Muffins

Corinne Gross
Tigard, OR

*I found this recipe in my grandmother's handwritten cookbook.
I remember eating these tasty muffins in the summertime when
Grandma's garden was overflowing with ripe, juicy tomatoes.*

1 c. all-purpose flour
1 c. whole-wheat flour
1/4 c. grated Parmesan cheese
2 T. sugar
1 T. baking powder
1/4 t. salt

1/2 t. dried oregano
1 egg, beaten
1 c. buttermilk
1/3 c. butter, melted
1 ripe tomato, coarsely chopped

In a bowl, combine flours, cheese, sugar, baking powder, salt and
oregano. Mix well. Stir in egg, buttermilk and butter just until blended.
Fold in tomato. Spoon batter into 12 paper-lined muffin cups, filling
3/4 full. Bake at 400 degrees for 20 minutes. Makes one dozen.

Look for heirloom vegetables at the farmers' market...old-timers that
Grandma knew and loved. With funny names like Country Gentleman
corn, Arkansas Traveler tomatoes, Calico Crowder peas and Jenny
Lind melons, they offer a delicious taste of the good old days.

Grandma's Johnny Cake

Shirley Howie
Foxboro, MA

My grandmother used to make this old New England favorite. We lived across the road from her. I remember going to visit her often and sharing a big warm piece of her johnnycake with lots of butter. She passed the recipe on to Mom and now I make it. It goes well with soups, stews and chili, and is also good with jam for breakfast.

3/4 c. all-purpose flour
1 t. baking soda
1/2 t. salt
2 T. sugar
1-1/4 c. yellow cornmeal

2 eggs, well beaten
1/4 c. white vinegar
1 c. evaporated milk
1/4 c. shortening, melted

In a bowl, mix flour, baking soda, salt and sugar well. Stir in cornmeal. In a separate bowl, stir together eggs, vinegar, evaporated milk and shortening. Add to flour mixture and stir just until moistened. Pour batter into a greased 8"x8" baking pan. Bake at 400 degrees for 30 to 35 minutes. Cut into squares; serve warm. Makes 6 to 8 servings.

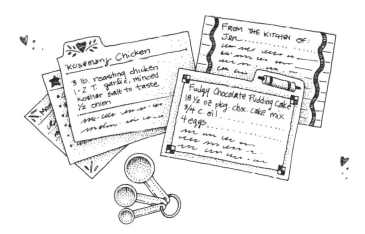

Take time to share family stories and traditions with your kids over the dinner table! A cherished family recipe can be a super conversation starter.

Mulligatawny Soup

Michelle Corning
Nova Scotia, Canada

My grandmother shared this old recipe with me. It's a chicken soup that gets its unusual flavor from apple and spices. I like to serve it with a basket of warm homemade rolls.

2 boneless, skinless chicken
  breasts
1 apple, cored and cubed
4 T. butter, sliced
1 c. onion, chopped
1 c. celery, chopped
1 c. carrots, peeled and diced
1 t. sugar
2 T. curry powder

1/2 t. ground mace
1/2 to 1 t. ground ginger
1 t. salt
1/2 t. pepper
14-1/2 oz. can crushed or
  diced tomatoes
8-oz. can tomato sauce
1 to 2 T. lemon juice

Cover chicken with water in a large saucepan. Cook over medium heat until chicken is tender, about 40 minutes. Set aside chicken to cool and dice; reserve broth in pan. Meanwhile, in a skillet over medium heat, sauté apple in butter. Add onion, celery, carrots, sugar, seasonings and enough water to cover vegetables. Simmer until vegetables are tender but not mushy. Add reserved chicken broth, tomatoes with juice and tomato sauce. Simmer for 40 minutes, stirring occasionally. Shortly before serving time, stir in chicken and lemon juice. Makes 6 to 7 servings.

Pass along Grandma's soup tureen to a new bride...fill it with favorite seasonings and tie on a cherished soup recipe.

Grandma's Pink Chicken Soup

Laura Huffstickler
Wadena, MN

My mother has made this chicken soup ever since I can remember. With 15 children, my grandmother had to feed an army everyday! This is one of her many recipes which she never wrote down. It's very hearty, tasty and different because of the pink coloring.

1-1/2 to 2 lbs. chicken
6 c. water
3 to 4 T. chicken soup base
2 potatoes, peeled and diced
1 onion, diced
2 carrots, peeled and sliced

1/2 to 1 head cabbage,
   thinly sliced
15-oz. can diced beets,
   drained
2 c. half-and-half
salt and pepper, if desired

Place chicken pieces in a kettle; add water. Cook over medium heat until chicken is tender, about 35 to 40 minutes. Remove chicken to a plate; reserve broth in kettle. Stir soup base into broth; add potatoes, onion and carrots. Simmer over low heat until vegetables are tender. Meanwhile, dice chicken, discarding bones and skin; set aside. When vegetables are tender, add cabbage and beets. Cook until cabbage is soft, about 15 minutes. Stir in chicken and half-and-half; warm through but do not boil. Makes 8 servings.

Grandma always used rich cream or half-and-half, often from her own dairy cows. Fat-free half-and-half can be substituted in cream soup recipes, for all the delicious flavor without the extra calories.

Yankee Chili

Kathleen Peters
Arlington, TX

I learned this recipe from my grandmother. Originally from Poland, she came to America and settled in Batavia, New York. A friend of hers there taught her to make this chili and it is truly my favorite. When a church I was attending in Dallas had a chili cook-off, everyone said my Yankee Chili didn't stand a chance...but it won!

2 lbs. ground beef
1 onion, chopped
1 green pepper, chopped
28-oz. can whole tomatoes
15-1/2 oz. can kidney beans
10-3/4 oz. can tomato soup

2 T. chili powder
2 t. dried cumin
2 t. paprika
Optional: shredded cheese,
   chopped onions, crackers,
   bread & butter

In a Dutch oven over medium-high heat, brown beef with onion and green pepper for 10 to 12 minutes. Drain; add tomatoes with juice, beans with juice, soup and seasonings. Stir to combine and bring to a boil. Turn heat to medium-low and simmer for one to 2 hours. Stir occasionally, breaking up whole tomatoes with the back of your spoon. Garnish as desired. Serves 6.

Granny's Jalapeño Cornbread

Tiffany Johnson
Grant, AL

No bowl of soup or chili is complete without cornbread! This recipe is delicious and easy to make.

1-1/4 c. cornmeal
1/2 t. baking soda
1/2 t. salt
2/3 c. buttermilk
1/3 c. oil

2 eggs, beaten
1 c. creamed corn
1 c. shredded Cheddar cheese
1 to 2 T. jalapeño peppers,
   chopped

In a bowl, mix cornmeal, baking soda and salt. In a separate bowl, mix buttermilk, oil and eggs. Stir into cornmeal mixture until most lumps are dissolved; don't overmix. Stir in remaining ingredients. Pour batter into a greased 13"x9" baking pan. Bake at 375 degrees for 30 to 40 minutes. Cut into squares. Makes 15 servings.

Hot Soup
to Warm You Up!

Ham & Lentil Soup

Megan Brooks
Antioch, TN

My Aunt Betty always had a pot of some kind of bean soup simmering on the back of her stove. Nowadays, I use a slow cooker...no standing over a hot stove! Sometimes I'll make this with a leftover ham bone. Just add it to the soup, then dice the meat.

3 c. chicken broth	1 onion, thinly sliced
3 c. water	1 c. dried lentils
1 c. cooked ham, diced	1-1/2 t. dried thyme
1-1/2 c. celery, chopped	3 c. fresh baby spinach
1-1/2 c. baby carrots, thinly sliced	Garnish shredded Parmesan cheese

In a 5-quart slow cooker, combine all ingredients except spinach and garnish. Stir well. Cover and cook on low setting for 7 to 8 hours. Stir in spinach; let stand for a few minutes, until wilted. Garnish each serving with a sprinkle of cheese. Makes 6 servings.

A cast-iron skillet is perfect for baking crisp, delicious cornbread.
Before you mix up the batter, drop a tablespoon of bacon drippings
or vegetable oil into the skillet and place it in the oven to preheat.
When the batter is ready, the skillet will be too.

Alphabet Vegetable Soup

Penny Sherman
Ava, MO

Whenever we visited my grandma on a chilly day, she'd have a pot of this soup ready to warm us up. I loved trying to find my name in the bowl of soup! If you're making it for grown-ups, it's fine to use pastina stars instead of alphabets.

1/3 c. oil	2 c. cabbage, finely shredded
1 c. onion, diced	1 c. frozen baby peas
8 c. beef or vegetable broth	1 bay leaf
15-oz. can whole tomatoes, cut up	salt and pepper to taste
2 to 3 carrots, peeled and thinly sliced	8-oz. pkg. alphabet pasta, uncooked

Heat oil in a large saucepan over medium heat. Add onion and cook until tender, stirring occasionally. Add broth, tomatoes with juice, vegetables and bay leaf. Bring to a boil; reduce heat to low. Simmer for 20 minutes. Season with salt and pepper. Stir pasta into soup; simmer for 8 minutes, or until pasta is tender. Discard bay leaf before serving. Serves 8.

Need to add a little zing to a pot of soup? Just add a splash of lemon juice or cider vinegar.

Hot Soup
to Warm You Up!

Chilled Gazpacho

Carrie O'Shea
Marina del Rey, CA

Gazpacho was popular in the 1970s when my grandmother first found this recipe. She often hosted luncheons for her women's club. This no-cook cold soup was always a hit in the summertime.

2 c. vegetable cocktail juice
3 lbs. ripe tomatoes, coarsely
    chopped
2 cucumbers, peeled and
    coarsely chopped
1 green pepper, coarsely
    chopped
1/2 c. sweet onion, coarsely
    chopped

2 to 3 cloves garlic, minced
1/3 c. olive oil
3 T. white wine vinegar
salt and pepper to taste
Optional: hot pepper sauce
    to taste
Garnish: seasoned croutons

In a large bowl, combine tomato juice, vegetables and garlic. Working in batches, transfer mixture to a blender. Process to desired consistency; pour into a separate large bowl. Stir in olive oil and vinegar; season with salt, pepper and hot sauce, if desired. Cover and chill. Serve in chilled bowls, topped with croutons. Serves 6.

Savory soup & salad croutons are easy to make. Toss cubes of
day-old bread with olive oil, garlic powder, salt and pepper.
Spread on a baking sheet in a single layer and bake at
400 degrees for about 10 minutes, until toasty.

Nanny's Shredded Wheat Bread

Wendi Knowles
Pittsfield, ME

My grandmother made this bread often. I remember spending time at her house and she would make toast for me with it. Whenever I bake this bread now, the aroma transports me back to her kitchen and the wonderful times I spent with her.

3 large shredded wheat biscuits
1/3 c. molasses
3 T. butter, sliced
1/4 c. sugar, divided
1 c. boiling water

1/2 c. warm water,
   110 to 115 degrees
2 T. active dry yeast
5 to 6 c. all-purpose flour,
   divided

Break up biscuits in a large bowl; add molasses, butter and 2 tablespoons sugar. Pour boiling water over all; stir. Let cool to room temperature. In a 2-cup measuring cup, dissolve yeast and remaining sugar in warm water. Let stand 5 minutes; add to biscuit mixture. Stir in 3 cups flour until well mixed. Continue to stir in flour until dough is smooth. Knead dough on a floured surface until smooth and elastic. Place dough in a greased bowl, turning to coat. Cover with a tea towel and let rise until double. Punch down dough; divide dough in half and place in 2 greased 9"x5" loaf pans. Cover and let rise again until double. Bake at 350 degrees for 35 to 40 minutes, until golden. Makes 2 loaves.

Grandma's little secret...kneading bread dough is a fun way to get rid of stress! Be sure to knead the dough as long as the recipe states, until the dough is silky smooth. You'll be rewarded with moist, tender bread.

Angel Biscuits

Lorrie Owens
Munford, TN

This is my grandmother's recipe. Just smelling these heavenly biscuits while they bake brings back wonderful memories.

1 env. active dry yeast	1 t. baking soda
2 T. warm water,	1 t. salt
110 to 115 degrees	1 c. shortening
5 c. all-purpose flour	2 c. buttermilk
3 T. sugar	Garnish: melted butter
3 T. baking powder	

In a cup, stir yeast into water until dissolved; set aside. In a large bowl, combine flour, sugar, baking powder, baking soda and salt; mix well. Add yeast mixture, shortening and buttermilk; stir well. Turn dough onto a floured surface and knead lightly. Roll out dough about 1/2-inch thick. Cut out with a 2" biscuit cutter. Place biscuits on an ungreased baking sheet; brush with melted butter. Bake at 400 degrees for 12 to 15 minutes, until lightly golden. Makes about 2-1/2 dozen.

Fresh-baked bread and biscuits are just asking for a pat of herb butter. Blend 1/2 cup softened butter and a teaspoon each of chopped fresh parsley, chives and dill. Spoon into a crock and keep chilled.

Grandma Shaffer's Scrap Soup

Marcia Shaffer
Conneaut Lake, PA

My grandma served this soup often to us. It's also called Perpetual Soup Pot. Whenever there are a lot of leftovers in the fridge, I like nothing better than to make my Scrap Soup. It is always different and usually delicious!

1 to 2 c. leftover cooked
    meat scraps
1 to 2 c. leftover vegetables,
    celery tops, chopped onion,
    mashed potatoes
3 to 5 cubes chicken or beef
    bouillon

5 c. water
dried thyme or other herbs
    to taste
salt and pepper to taste
Optional: cooked egg noodles,
    rice or couscous

Chop up scraps into bite-size pieces. Combine all except optional ingredients in a 5-quart slow cooker. Cover and cook on low setting for 6 to 8 hours. Stir in cooked noodles, rice or couscous, if desired. Serves 6 to 8.

Corn Fritters

Bethi Hendrickson
Danville. PA

When I was growing up in central Pennsylvania, these fritters were a staple in our country home. They're not only quick to make, but so yummy.

2 c. fresh or frozen corn,
    cooked
1 egg, beaten
1 T. baking powder

2 c. all-purpose flour
1 T. sugar
1 t. salt
shortening for frying

In a bowl, combine corn, egg and baking powder. In a separate bowl, mix remaining ingredients. Add flour mixture to corn mixture; stir until moistened. Melt shortening 1/2-inch deep in a skillet over medium-high heat. With a small cookie scoop, add batter to skillet, a few at a time. Cook about 5 minutes on each side, until golden. Drain on a paper towel-lined plate until ready to serve. Makes one dozen.

Eat
Your
Veggies,
Dear

Helen's Wilted Lettuce Salad

Dawn Raskiewicz
Alliance, NE

*I grew up in Oregon and our next-door neighbor was named Helen.
She was our proxy Grandma, as she used to say. This recipe is hers.
Whenever I make this salad, I think about her and remember all the
fun times we had. Fresh leaf lettuce from the garden is best for this.*

1 head leaf lettuce, cut into
   bite-sized pieces
1/4 c. green onions, thinly sliced
1 T. fresh herbs such as chives
   and parsley, snipped
5 slices bacon, diced
1/4 c. vinegar
1-1/2 t. sugar

1 t. dry mustard
1/8 t. garlic salt
1/4 t. salt
1/4 t. pepper
2 eggs, hard-boiled, peeled
   and chopped
Garnish: paprika

In a salad bowl, combine lettuce, onions and herbs; set aside. In a
skillet over medium heat, cook bacon until crisp. Drain, reserving
1/4 cup drippings. Crumble bacon and add to salad bowl. In a
saucepan over medium heat, combine reserved drippings, vinegar,
sugar and seasonings. Bring to a boil, stirring occasionally. Pour hot
dressing over salad; toss well. Sprinkle chopped eggs on top. Add a
dash of paprika to the eggs. Serve at once. Makes 4 servings.

A well-used wooden salad bowl is a terrific find. To restore
the bowl's glowing finish, sand lightly inside and out with
fine sandpaper. Rub a little vegetable oil over the bowl and
let stand overnight, then wipe off any excess oil.

Shoepeg Corn Salad

Opal McCoy
Fort Gibson, OK

This recipe was handed down to my family from a dear friend of my mother's. It is a very colorful salad we enjoy every 4th of July and again at Christmas. You may add any additional vegetables to this.

3 11-oz. cans shoepeg corn,
    drained
4-oz. jar diced pimentos, drained
2-1/4 oz. can chopped black
    olives, drained
3 to 4 green onions, chopped
1 green pepper, diced

1 stalk celery, chopped
1 c. mayonnaise
1 c. ranch salad dressing
1 T. dried parsley
2 t. garlic powder
salt and pepper to taste

In a large bowl, combine all vegetables; toss to mix. In a small bowl, combine mayonnaise, salad dressing and seasonings. Pour dressing over vegetables and mix well. Cover and chill at least 3 hours before serving. Makes 12 servings.

An old straw shopping tote makes a whimsical planter
for marigolds and zinnias. Just slip it over a fence post
and fill with potted flowers.

Stuffed Tomatoes

Ruth Downour
Union Furnace, OH

This recipe is filled with lovely memories. It was one of my grandmother's and mom's. My grandmother also raised me.

1 green pepper, diced
1 cucumber, diced
1 onion, diced
16-oz. container small-curd
   cottage cheese, well drained

1/2 c. Green Goddess salad
   dressing
4 large ripe tomatoes
Garnish: leaf lettuce
salt and pepper to taste

Place pepper, cucumber and onion in a large bowl. Add cottage cheese; mix well. Stir in salad dressing; set aside. Core each tomato from the top. Slice tomatoes from top to almost the bottom to create several wedges that open up like a flower. Line 4 salad plates with lettuce; place a tomato on each plate. Spoon vegetable mixture into the center of each tomato. Season with salt and pepper. Cover and chill until serving time. Makes 4 servings.

Sweet & Juicy Tomatoes

Claudia Ohl
Covington, IN

My mom made these tomatoes from the time I was a little girl... always a favorite with my brothers and me. The sugar really brings the juices out.

3 to 4 ripe tomatoes, peeled and
   cubed

1 to 2 T. sugar
salt and pepper to taste

Place tomatoes in a bowl. Sprinkle with sugar and seasonings; toss gently. Cover and chill for 30 minutes before serving. Serves 4 to 6.

To speed ripening, place tomatoes in a brown paper bag in a dark closet. The tomatoes will ripen overnight.

Eat Your Veggies, *Dear*

Pickled Beets & Eggs

Cathy Needham
Columbus, OH

This is my mother-in-law Marie's recipe. Our copy is handwritten by both my husband Dan and me, from what she told us. In later years she made it with sugar substitute. She never added all the beet juice from each can, but we do, as we like the extra color it gives.

3 c. white vinegar
2 c. water
2-1/2 c. sugar
2 t. whole allspice
1/2 t. whole cloves

1 t. salt
3-inch cinnamon stick
5 15-oz. cans small whole beets
6 to 8 eggs, hard-boiled and
  peeled

In a large saucepan over medium-high heat, combine all ingredients except beets and eggs. Bring to a boil. Reduce heat to medium-low and simmer for 15 minutes, stirring occasionally. Add beets with juice; simmer for 5 minutes. Remove from heat. Add peeled hard-boiled eggs to pan, pushing gently into liquid. Cover and refrigerate overnight before serving. Eggs may be halved for serving. Serves 8 to 10.

Grandma's Cucumbers

Crystal Willich
Horton, KS

My grandma used to fix cucumbers this way every summer... they were always so delicious!

6 cucumbers, peeled and sliced
1 onion, thinly sliced
1 c. mayonnaise
1/3 c. sugar

2 T. vinegar
pepper to taste
Garnish: 1/4 t. dill weed,
  if desired

In a bowl, combine sliced cucumbers and onion. In another small bowl, mix together remaining ingredients. Pour over cucumber mixture; stir well. Sprinkle dill weed over salad, if using. Cover and refrigerate several hours before serving. Makes 4 to 6 servings.

Grandma's Layered Cabbage Salad

Melissa Dattoli
Richmond, VA

My grandma makes this delicious salad and it's a staple at our family gatherings. I've brought it to many potlucks too, and people always ask for the recipe. It is a great summertime side, perfect for a hot day.

1 head green cabbage, shredded
   and divided
1 sweet onion, chopped
1 green pepper, chopped
1 c. sugar

1/2 c. oil
1 c. white vinegar
1/2 t. celery seed
1 t. salt

In a large bowl, layer half of the cabbage with all of the onion and pepper; add remaining cabbage. Sprinkle sugar over top; do not stir. In a small saucepan over medium heat, combine remaining ingredients. Bring to a full boil, stirring well. Pour hot mixture over cabbage mixture; do not stir. Cover and refrigerate overnight. Just before serving, stir salad well. Makes 12 servings.

Make a cut-glass serving tray sparkle like diamonds...it's easy!
Wash it in mild dish soap, then rinse well with a mixture that's
half plain warm water and half white vinegar. Pat dry with
a lint-free towel...that's all it takes.

Mom's Macaroni Salad

Krista Marshall
Fort Wayne, IN

This recipe has been passed down from my grandma to my mom and now to me. It's our favorite version, and so simple. It's perfect for barbecues, cook-outs and picnics. Be sure to use mayonnaise-type salad dressing...mayonnaise just doesn't taste the same!

16-oz. pkg. rotini pasta,
   uncooked
6 eggs, hard-boiled, peeled
   and chopped
10-oz. jar green olives, drained
   and sliced
1/2 c. onion, finely chopped

1-1/2 c. mayonnaise-type salad
   dressing
3 T. mustard
3 T. sweet pickle relish
1 t. celery seed
salt and pepper to taste
Garnish: paprika

Cook pasta according to package directions; drain and rinse with cold water. In a large bowl, combine cooked pasta, eggs, olives and onion. In a small bowl, whisk together remaining ingredients except garnish. Pour dressing over pasta mixture. Stir well to combine. Cover and chill until serving, at least 2 hours. At serving time, stir again and sprinkle with paprika. Makes 8 to 10 servings.

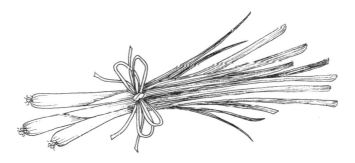

Whip up some tangy green onion dressing for a simple lettuce salad. Blend 1/3 cup mayonnaise, 1/4 cup sour cream, one tablespoon milk, one teaspoon lemon juice and 2 finely chopped green onions. How easy!

Fresh Broccoli Salad

Donna Hungerford
Aurora, CO

My mom used to make broccoli salad often in the summertime. Now, whenever I go to a salad bar, broccoli salad is the first thing I put on my plate to see if I like the blend of ingredients!

2 bunches broccoli, finely chopped
1 c. sharp Cheddar cheese, shredded or diced
1 onion, chopped
10 slices bacon, crisply cooked and chopped
1/4 to 1/2 c. sunflower seed kernels

3/4 to 1 c. mayonnaise or mayonnaise-style salad dressing
3 to 4 T. sugar or sugar substitute
3 to 4 T. white vinegar
salt or salt-free seasoning and pepper to taste

In a large bowl, combine broccoli, cheese, onion, bacon and sunflower seeds. In a small bowl, combine remaining ingredients. Pour dressing over broccoli mixture; mix to coat well. Cover and refrigerate until serving time. Serves 6 to 10.

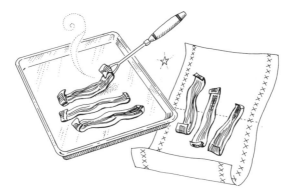

Prepare lots of crispy bacon easily...bake it! Place bacon slices on a broiler pan. Bake at 400 degrees for 12 to 15 minutes. Turn bacon over and bake for another 8 to 10 minutes. Toss on a few extra slices for your next BLT!

Eat
Your Veggies,
Dear

Sharon's Freezer Slaw

Lori Peterson
Effingham, KS

I've always heard my grandma and my mother-in-law talk about Freezer Slaw. But I'd never tasted it myself until recently, when my mother-in-law Sharon made some. I was hesitant about trying it, but when I did, I fell in love with it! I like to spoon it into plastic whipped topping containers. It fills a little over four of them.

1 head cabbage, finely shredded	1 t. salt
1 carrot, peeled and finely	1 c. white vinegar
shredded	1/4 c. water
1 green pepper, finely diced	2 c. sugar
Optional: 1 red pepper, finely	1 t. celery seed
diced	1 t. mustard seed

Combine vegetables in a bowl; sprinkle with salt. Let stand for one hour; drain and press out excess liquid. In a saucepan over medium heat, combine remaining ingredients. Boil for one minute, stirring until sugar dissolves; cool completely. Pour over cabbage mixture; stir well. Divide slaw among plastic containers; cover and freeze. Thaw in the refrigerator before serving. Makes about 4 pints.

Simple Coleslaw

Joanne Mauseth
Reno, NV

My mom would add little surprises to her coleslaw from time to time. Some of her favorites were raisins and diced bits of apple.

1 head cabbage, shredded	1 to 2 T. vinegar
3/4 c. sugar	5-oz. can evaporated milk

Place cabbage in a large salad bowl; sprinkle with sugar. Add vinegar, using more if you like a little extra tartness. Let stand until sugar dissolves, about 30 minutes. Add evaporated milk and mix well. Cover and chill until serving time. Serves 10 to 15.

Cardinal Chicken Salad

Shirl Parsons
Cape Carteret, NC

This recipe comes from Granny Thelma Skelton, my husband's grandmother. She was a great cook and entertained often.

2 c. apples, cored and finely
   chopped
1 T. lemon juice
4 c. cooked chicken, finely
   chopped
1-1/2 c. celery, finely chopped

1/2 t. salt
1/4 t. pepper
1-1/4 c. mayonnaise, divided
8-oz. pkg. cream cheese,
   softened

Place apples in a large bowl; sprinkle with lemon juice and toss well. Add chicken, celery, salt and pepper; toss again. Add 3/4 cup mayonnaise and mix lightly. Press mixture into a 1-1/2 quart bowl or salad mold. Cover and chill several hours. Shortly before serving time, unmold onto a serving platter. Blend cream cheese with remaining mayonnaise; spread over salad mold. Serves 6.

Try poaching for juicy, tender chicken. Cover boneless, skinless chicken breasts with water in a saucepan. Bring to a boil. Turn down the heat, cover and simmer over low heat for 10 to 12 minutes, until chicken is no longer pink in the center.

Judy's Deviled Eggs

Judy Taylor
Butler, MO

My granddaughter told me she loves my "Doubled Eggs" as she calls them. Feel free to adjust the amounts to suit your preference for seasoning and consistency.

1 doz. eggs, hard-boiled, peeled
    and halved lengthwise
1/2 c. mayonnaise
1 T. sugar
3 T. sweet pickle juice

1 T. mustard
1/4 t. salt
1/4 t. white pepper
Garnish: paprika

Separate egg whites from yolks; arrange whites on a platter and set aside. Mash egg yolks in a bowl with a fork. Add remaining ingredients except garnish; whip until smooth. Spoon filling into egg whites; sprinkle with paprika. Cover and refrigerate until serving time. Makes 2 dozen.

For the nicest looking hard-boiled eggs, use eggs that have been refrigerated at least 7 to 10 days, instead of fresher eggs. After boiling and cooling in ice water, the eggshells will slip right off.

Peacock Potato Salad

Linda Clark
Emmitsburg, MD

My daughter and I always choose this potato salad as a part of our birthday meal. It is one of my mother's favorite recipes. She said it came from my Grandmother Buffington, whom I never knew. I always wondered about its name. Years later, when doing my family tree, I found the name of my great-grandmother...Margaret Peacock. The mystery was solved!

8 potatoes, peeled and cubed
1/2 c. sugar
1 t. cornstarch
1 t. dry mustard
1/8 t. salt
1 egg, beaten
1/2 c. vinegar

1/2 c. water
1 T. butter
1/2 t. celery seed
1 onion, diced
1 T. fresh parsley, snipped
2 T. mayonnaise

Cover potatoes with water in a large saucepan. Cook over high heat until tender; drain and rinse with cool water. In a bowl, mix together sugar, cornstarch, mustard, salt and egg; set aside. In a small saucepan over medium heat, bring vinegar, water and butter to a boil. Slowly add sugar mixture to vinegar mixture; stir. Return pan to low heat; cook and stir until thickened. Add celery seed; cool. Add sauce, onion, parsley and mayonnaise to potatoes; mix well. Chill. Serves 8.

No-Mayo Potato Salad

Gretchen Arnason
Berkeley, CA

I've never cared for the taste of mayonnaise, so my Grandma Rue started making this just for me!

5 redskin potatoes, halved
2 zesty dill pickle spears, diced
1/2 onion, diced

4-oz. can sliced green olives, drained and diced
Italian salad dressing to taste

Place potatoes in a large saucepan; cover with water. Bring to a boil over high heat. Boil until fork-tender; drain and chill completely. Dice potatoes; place in a salad bowl. Add remaining ingredients and toss to mix. Serve chilled. Makes 6 to 8 servings.

Simple Squash & Onions

Cindy McKinnon
El Dorado, AR

My grandparents used to fix this dish for me. I loved it then and now I fix it often for my family. It is so good in summertime when squash is abundant.

2 to 3 T. bacon drippings or oil
8 to 10 yellow squash, chopped
1 onion, chopped
salt and pepper to taste
2 T. butter, sliced
1/4 c. sugar

Add drippings or oil to a large skillet over medium-high heat. Add squash and onion; season with salt and pepper. Stir; reduce heat to medium-low. Add butter. Cover and cook about 30 minutes, stirring often, until squash is tender. Stir in sugar. Serves 6 to 8.

Sautéed Zucchini & Yellow Squash

Andrea Snyder
Carterville, IL

When I was growing up, my mother always used to make this dish for us. I have continued to make it for my children, who often have a second helping or three! It is so good and quick.

3 T. butter
2 to 3 zucchini and/or yellow
   squash, thinly sliced
2 cloves garlic, minced
1/2 c. grated Parmesan cheese

Melt butter in a skillet over medium heat. Add squash; sprinkle with garlic. Stir; sauté until crisp-tender. If desired, cover to speed up cooking a little. Just before serving sprinkle with cheese. Let stand until melted. Makes 4 servings.

Every house needs a grandmother in it.

— Louisa May Alcott

Farmhouse Garden Slaw

Christine Gordon
Derby, KS

During our summer trips to the farm as kids, I remember helping Grandma toss together this yummy slaw to go with just about any meal we shared. It was a great way for Grandma to get us to eat our veggies, and also to help her use up some of her garden's bounty! We also would add other veggies as they became in season, like red and yellow bell peppers, heirloom tomatoes and fresh green beans.

1 head green cabbage, thinly
   sliced and separated, or
   14-oz. pkg. coleslaw mix
1 to 2 tomatoes, diced

1 cucumber, diced
1/4 to 1/2 c. onion, finely diced
8-oz. bottle ranch salad dressing
salt and pepper to taste

Combine cabbage, tomatoes, cucumber and onion in a large salad bowl. Add enough salad dressing to coat everything well. Season with salt and pepper. Mix well. Makes 8 servings.

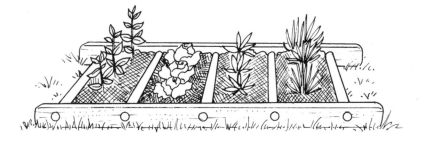

Try your hand at vegetable gardening! Even the smallest yard is sure to have a sunny corner where you can grow sun-ripened tomatoes and an herb plant or two. Seeds, plants and free advice are available at the nearest garden store.

3-Bean Basil Salad

April Jacobs
Loveland, CO

*Fresh vegetables and basil from your garden will make
this wonderful side dish even better!*

2 c. canned no-salt kidney
   beans, rinsed
2 c. canned no-salt chickpeas,
   rinsed
2 c. canned no-salt green beans,
   rinsed
1 red onion, sliced and separated
   into rings
1 carrot, peeled and grated

1/2 c. vinegar
1/4 c. canola oil
3 T. sugar
1 T. fresh basil, minced
3/4 t. dry mustard
1/4 t. salt
1/2 t. pepper
Garnish: fresh basil leaves

Combine beans, onion and carrot in a large bowl. Combine remaining
ingredients except garnish in a small bowl and mix well; pour over
bean mixture and toss well. Cover and refrigerate overnight; serve
chilled. Garnish with basil leaves if desired. Makes 12 servings.

Headed for a picnic in the country? It's simple to tote a salad. Mix it
up in a plastic zipping bag, seal and set it right in the cooler. When you
arrive at the picnic grounds, simply tip the salad into a serving bowl.

Secret-Recipe Shrimp Salad

Donna Guthrie
North Benton, OH

This recipe was my girlfriend's family secret for over 50 years. It is excellent for potlucks and family gatherings...you will bring home an empty bowl! Add some chopped onion, if you like.

16-oz. pkg. elbow macaroni, uncooked
1-1/2 lbs. small shrimp, cooked and cleaned
16-oz. pkg. frozen peas, thawed
8 stalks celery, finely chopped
1-1/3 c. mayonnaise

3/4 c. French salad dressing
2 T. sugar
2 T. white wine vinegar
1-1/2 to 2-1/2 t. paprika
2 t. garlic powder
2 t. salt
1 t. pepper

Cook macaroni according to package directions. Drain; rinse with cool water and transfer to a large serving bowl. Add shrimp, peas and celery; mix together. In a separate bowl, whisk together remaining ingredients. Pour dressing over salad; toss gently. Cover and refrigerate overnight. Serves 16.

Vintage magazine recipe ads make fun wall art for the kitchen. They're easy to find at flea markets. Look for ones featuring shimmery gelatin salads, golden macaroni & cheese or other favorites like Grandma used to make!

Marinated Tomatoes

JoAnn
Gooseberry Patch

I love going into the garden to pick sun-warmed heirloom tomatoes
for our supper. This recipe is a simple trick to make them even tastier.

3 to 4 ripe tomatoes, thickly
    sliced
1/3 c. olive oil
1/4 c. red wine vinegar
salt to taste

1/4 t. pepper
1/2 clove garlic, minced
2 T. onion, chopped
1 T. fresh parsley, minced
1 T. fresh basil, minced

Arrange tomato slices in a large shallow dish; set aside. In a small
bowl, whisk together remaining ingredients. Drizzle dressing over
tomatoes. Pour over tomato slices. Cover and chill for several hours
before serving. Makes 6 to 8 servings.

Keep a bunch of fresh green parsley in the fridge, ready to add
a little color and a taste of the garden to meals anytime. Simply
place the bunch, stems down, in a glass of water and cover
the top loosely with a plastic sandwich bag.

Dad's Favorite Fruit Salad

Carolyn Deckard
Bedford, IN

Mom made this fruit salad for Dad for many, many years.
It was his favorite...all of us kids liked it too. Mix & match
other combinations of fruit as you like.

1/2 head lettuce, torn
1 c. seedless green grapes
2 doz. melon balls
3 peaches, halved, pitted
   and sliced

3 bananas, sliced
6-oz. can frozen orange juice
   concentrate, divided
1 c. vanilla or plain yogurt
1 T. honey

Place lettuce in a large salad bowl; add fruit and set aside. Add half of orange juice concentrate to a separate bowl; reserve remaining concentrate for another recipe. Add yogurt and honey; whisk well and drizzle over fruit. Cover and refrigerate. Serves 6.

For the tastiest fruit salads, choose the ripest seasonal fresh fruits instead of ones that have been shipped a long distance. Add a sprinkle of orange zest or chopped mint to punch up flavor.

Ginger Ale Salad

*Betty Gretch
Owendale, MI*

*This is an old-fashioned recipe that my mom had for many years.
I often make it for Easter because it is a light salad that
goes well with baked ham.*

1/2 c. boiling water
3-oz. pkg. lemon gelatin mix
1-1/3 c. ginger ale, chilled
1 c. seedless red grapes, halved

11-oz. can mandarin oranges,
    drained
11-oz. can pineapple tidbits,
    drained

In a bowl, add boiling water to gelatin mix; stir until dissolved. Stir in
ginger ale; cover and chill. When gelatin begins to thicken, stir in fruit.
Cover and chill 2 to 3 hours, until completely set. Serves 8.

Uncle Jesse's Ambrosia Salad

*Ramona Wysong
Barlow, KY*

*My grandmother Fanny Hook made this yummy salad for
my Uncle Jesse. Refrigerate overnight for the best flavor.*

11-oz. can mandarin oranges,
    drained and chopped
11-oz. can crushed pineapple,
    drained
1/2 to 1 c. flaked coconut

3 to 4 c. mini marshmallows
8-oz. container sour cream
Optional: 14-1/2 oz. jar
    maraschino cherries

Combine all ingredients in a bowl, adding desired amounts of coconut
and marshmallows. Stir to moisten well with sour cream. Cover and
refrigerate overnight before serving. Serves 8.

Fruity gelatin salads are yummy
when topped with a dollop of creamy
lemon mayonnaise. To 1/2 cup
mayonnaise, add 3 tablespoons
each of lemon juice, light cream
and powdered sugar.

Skillet-Fried Sweet Corn

Tina George
El Dorado, AR

This is a recipe my grandma made every time she came to visit. Ma would stay with us for up to two weeks at a time and she cooked the whole time she was there! Momma would help her, of course, but Ma preferred to be "in charge" in the kitchen. We did our best not to get in the way. Oh, how I miss her.

5 to 6 ears sweet corn
1-1/2 T. bacon drippings
   or butter
2 T. milk

2 to 3 t. sugar to taste
1/2 t. salt
pepper to taste

Using a knife, cut corn kernels from cobs; set kernels aside in a bowl. With the knife or a spoon, scrape in a downward motion, removing remaining corn from cobs. Set aside scrapings with kernels. Melt drippings or butter in a skillet over medium-high heat. When drippings melt and begin to sizzle, add corn to skillet. Reduce heat to medium. Cook for 15 to 20 minutes, stirring often. Add milk; stir. Sprinkle with sugar, salt and pepper. Stir until combined and heated through. Serve warm. Makes 4 servings.

When cutting the kernels from ears of sweet corn, stand the ear in the center of a tube cake pan. The kernels will fall neatly into the pan.

Sweet Fried Green Tomatoes

Kandace Giles
Sylacauga, AL

This recipe is half mine and half my grandmother's. One night we were having dinner at her house and she was making fried green tomatoes. Instead of grabbing the flour, she grabbed pancake mix! These turned out to be a sweeter version of the usual fried green tomatoes...so delicious!

1 c. cornmeal	2 eggs
1 c. pancake mix	4 green tomatoes, sliced to
1 T. salt	desired thickness
1 T. pepper	oil for frying

In a large bowl, mix together cornmeal, pancake mix, salt and pepper; set aside. Beat eggs in a separate large bowl. Dip each tomato slice into eggs, add to cornmeal mixture and coat tomatoes on both sides. To a large skillet over medium heat, add 1/2-inch oil. Add 4 to 5 coated tomatoes to oil at a time; cook until golden on both sides. Remove tomatoes to a paper towel-lined plate. Let cool about 2 minutes before serving. Serves 4.

For a fresh change from spinach, give Swiss chard a try.
An old-timey favorite that probably grew in your grandmother's garden, it's easy to prepare too. Just steam until tender, then drizzle with cider vinegar to taste.

Creamy Mashed Potatoes

Lori Simmons
Princeville, IL

I was raised on homemade mashed potatoes and still make them for my family. They're so much more flavorful than instant!

3 to 4 potatoes, peeled and
   cubed
1/4 c. butter, softened

1/4 c. milk
1/4 t. salt
1/8 t. pepper

Cover potatoes with water in a saucepan over medium-high heat. Boil until tender; drain. Mash potatoes until creamy. Stir in remaining ingredients until well blended. Serves 4.

Great-Gram's Mashed Potato Balls

Sandy Coffey
Cincinnati, OH

A delicious way to use leftover mashed potatoes. Great with cheeseburgers and a tossed salad!

2 c. cold mashed potatoes
1 egg yolk, beaten

salt and pepper to taste
Garnish: butter to taste

In a bowl, blend mashed potatoes with egg yolk; season with salt and pepper. Shape mixture into golfball-size balls. Place balls on a greased baking sheet; make a well in the top of each. Add a pat of butter to each well. Bake at 400 degrees for about 15 minutes, until golden. Serves 4.

For perfect mashed potatoes, boil potatoes until fork-tender. Drain, then return to the pan and shake dry over very low heat. Add a little warmed milk and softened butter, then mash to desired texture...don't overmash! Season with salt, pepper and extra butter to taste. Yum!

Slow-Simmered Green Beans

Diana Chaney
Olathe, KS

To me, there's nothing better than green beans from the garden! Mom shared this recipe with me. She said she remembers sitting on the porch with her grandmother, snapping the ends off green beans and chatting about this & that.

2 lbs. fresh green beans, trimmed
1 red onion, chopped
1 tomato, chopped
1/2 c. olive oil
juice of 1 lemon
2 cloves garlic, minced
2/3 c. water
salt and pepper to taste

Combine all ingredients in a Dutch oven or soup pot. Cover and cook over medium-low heat for about 2 hours, stirring occasionally, until beans are extremely tender. If liquid is cooking off too quickly, reduce heat to low and add a little more water. Serve hot or at room temperature. Serves 4 to 6.

Mix up some herbal vinegar. Fill a Mason jar with a cup of finely chopped fresh herbs like parsley, chives, basil and dill. Pour in 2 cups white wine vinegar, heated just to boiling. Cap the jar and let stand for 3 weeks, shaking it gently now and then. Strain and use it to jazz up salads and steamed veggies.

Hough-Pough

Bev Weeks
New Brunswick, Canada

This is a dish my great-grandmother made...real comfort food! She used all fresh-picked vegetables, including carrots and potatoes just pulled from the ground. Serve with meat or fish, hot dinner rolls, sliced tomatoes and cukes for a wonderful homestyle meal.

3 lbs. baby redskin potatoes,
    halved as needed
2 c. baby carrots
2 c. fresh green peas, shelled
2 c. fresh yellow wax beans,
    snapped

2 c. fresh green beans,
    snapped
2 c. whole milk
1 c. heavy cream
1/4 c. butter, sliced

Combine all vegetables in a large stew pot; cover with cold water. Bring to a full boil over high heat. Reduce heat to low. Cover and simmer gently for about 20 minutes, until vegetables are fork-tender. Drain and return vegetables to pot. Add milk, cream and butter. Cook over very low heat until heated through; do not boil. Makes 8 servings.

Serve up a veggie plate for dinner...a good old southern tradition that's perfect for lighter meals. With 2 or 3 scrumptious veggie dishes and a basket of buttery biscuits or cornbread, no one will miss the meat!

Bohemian Sauerkraut

Nancy Sharp
Chula Vista, CA

A lot of people don't like sauerkraut because of the bitterness. But you'll love this! From the Tesar family tradition...my family grew up in a little town by the lake called Sawyer, Michigan. My dad was Bohemian and my mom was Polish. We would make this sweet and flavorful family recipe to go with pork roast and big bread dumplings.

32-oz. jar refrigerated
   sauerkraut
10-3/4 oz. can cream of
   chicken soup

1/4 c. brown sugar, packed
4 slices bacon, crisply cooked
   and crumbled
3 T. caraway seed

Rinse and drain sauerkraut in a colander; transfer to a saucepan. Add remaining ingredients; bring to a simmer over low heat. Cook for one hour, stirring every 10 minutes or so. Makes 6 servings.

Are your hands dry and rough after preparing a meal? Mix it up yourself like Grandma did. Combine one teaspoon each of vegetable oil, lemon juice and honey. Rub it into your hands and wait 10 minutes, then rinse with warm water.

Mema Jeanette's Baked Corn

Cindy Kemp
Lake Jackson, TX

Absolutely decadent! I first tasted this bit of heaven in 2002 at my husband's step-mother's home. Mema Jeanette completely stole my heart with her gentle, kind ways and, of course, her amazing cooking skills. Mema has gone on to be with the Lord, but every time I make this side dish, every member of the family smiles at her wonderful memory. Fresh corn is really the best for this!

8 to 10 ears sweet corn
1/2 c. butter, sliced
16-oz. pkg. frozen creamed
   corn, thawed, or 14-3/4 oz.
   can creamed corn
1/4 c. sugar

2 T. all-purpose flour
salt and pepper to taste
1 c. half-and-half or milk
Optional: additional
   1/2 c. butter, melted

Cut kernels from cobs and blanch in boiling water. Drain; transfer to a large bowl and set aside. Place butter in a 2-quart casserole dish; set in the oven at 350 degrees, until melted. Meanwhile, add creamed corn, sugar, flour, seasonings and half-and-half or milk to corn. Mix well, being careful not to mash the corn. Carefully remove casserole dish from oven; pour corn mixture into dish. If desired, drizzle with additional butter. Bake, uncovered, at 350 degrees for 45 to 50 minutes, until bubbly and edges are golden. Remove from oven and let stand for about 20 minutes, until thickened slightly. Makes 6 to 8 servings.

Blanching makes fresh vegetables crisp and bright-colored.
Bring a large saucepan of salted water to a rolling boil. Add trimmed veggies and boil for 3 to 4 minutes, just until they begin to soften.
Immediately drain and cover veggies with ice water.
Cool, drain and pat dry.

Broccoli-Corn Casserole

Melanie Springer
Canton, OH

My mom used to make this tasty side dish for holiday dinners.
It is a favorite of all who try it. I make it, my kids make it and
I have shared this recipe with so many people.

10-oz. pkg. frozen chopped
   broccoli, thawed and
   squeezed dry
16-oz. can creamed corn
1 egg, beaten

1 T. minced dried onion
salt and pepper to taste
3 T. butter, melted and divided
18 saltine crackers, coarsely
   crushed and divided

In a bowl, combine broccoli, creamed corn, egg, onion, seasonings,
2 tablespoons melted butter and 2/3 of cracker crumbs. Mix well;
transfer to a greased one-quart casserole dish. In a small bowl; toss
together remaining cracker crumbs and butter; sprinkle over casserole.
Bake, uncovered, at 350 degrees for about 40 minutes, until hot and
bubbly. For a double or triple recipe, use a 13"x9" baking pan; bake
about 50 minutes. May be made ahead and reheated. Serves 4.

Pick up a vintage divided serving dish or two. They're just right for
serving up a choice of veggie sides without crowding the table.

Taylor-Made Wild Rice Casserole

Judy Taylor
Butler, MO

The first time my husband took me to visit his grandparents, Grandma Goldie Taylor made this delicious casserole for us. I had never been a fan of wild rice until I tasted this. It is especially good with a roasted Thanksgiving turkey.

6-oz. pkg. long-grain &
   wild rice mix
1 green pepper, chopped
4-oz. can mushroom pieces,
   drained

1 onion, chopped
1/2 c. margarine
8-oz. pkg. American cheese,
   chopped
1 c. half-and-half

Prepare rice according to package directions. Meanwhile, in a skillet over medium heat, sauté green pepper, mushrooms and onion in margarine. Layer rice and vegetable mixture in a greased 2-quart casserole dish; sprinkle cheese on top. Pour half-and-half over all. Bake, uncovered, at 400 degrees for 30 minutes. Serves 8.

Dale's Rice Dish

Melissa Scott
O'Fallon, MO

This recipe is perfect for the family get-togethers. It's been a favorite of my daughter for 16 years.

4 c. instant rice, uncooked
1 lb. bacon
1 bunch green onions, diced

7-oz. can mushroom stems &
   pieces, drained
soy sauce to taste

Prepare rice according to package directions. Meanwhile, cook bacon in a skillet over medium heat until crisp. Drain and chop bacon; reserve some drippings in pan. Stir onions and mushrooms into drippings; simmer until tender. Add cooked rice and bacon to skillet. Stir in enough soy sauce to turn mixture brown. Simmer until heated through. Serves 8 to 10.

Eat
Your Veggies,
Dear

Speedy Spanish Rice

Andrea Heyart
Savannah, TX

My mother-in-law gave me this easy recipe years ago and I still make it at least once a month. Sometimes I like to switch it up and add green chiles or corn and cilantro, for a little Texas flair!

3/4 c. onion, diced
1/4 c. oil
1-1/2 c. instant rice, uncooked

10-oz. can tomato sauce
1-1/2 c. chicken broth
salt and pepper to taste

In a skillet over medium heat, sauté onion in oil until translucent. Add uncooked rice, tomato sauce and chicken broth. Reduce heat to low. Cover and cook until rice is tender and liquid has evaporated. Season with salt and pepper. Serves 4 to 6.

Spanish Zucchini

Joyce Brewer
Mount Sterling, KY

This was one of my mother's recipes that she made for her family. She was a great cook! I'm happy to pass it on for her, we love it so.

1/2 c. onion, chopped
1/2 c. celery, chopped
1/4 c. green pepper, chopped
1/4 c. butter, sliced

2 c. zucchini, chopped
1 c. canned diced tomatoes
1/2 t. salt

In a skillet over medium heat, sauté onion, celery and green pepper in butter. Add zucchini, tomatoes and salt. Cover and cook over medium-low heat for 20 to 25 minutes. Makes 6 servings.

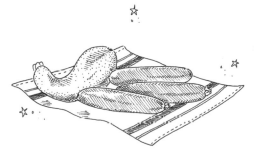

Try substituting old-fashioned yellow crookneck or pattypan squash for zucchini in any favorite recipe.

Gramma's Baked Beans

Scarlett Hedden
Port Saint John, FL

Gramma was from Boston, so I'm almost positive this recipe is authentic for New England baked beans. It has been passed down to me and I make it for holidays, picnics and potlucks. It takes a little time, but what dish doesn't, if it's really good?

1 lb. dried navy beans
1 c. unsulphured molasses
1 c. brown sugar, packed
1 yellow onion, diced

1 t. Worcestershire sauce
1 t. Dijon mustard
1/2 t. salt
1/4 lb. salt pork, sliced

Place beans in a large Dutch oven; cover with water. Soak for 4 hours. Drain; return beans to Dutch oven. Add enough fresh water to cover beans. Bring to a boil over high heat. Reduce heat to medium-low. Cover and cook for about 45 minutes, just until tender. Drain, reserving liquid. In a bowl, combine remaining ingredients except salt pork. Place 1/3 of beans in a lightly greased 2-quart bean pot; add a small amount of reserved liquid. Cover with 1/3 of molasses mixture; top with 1/3 of salt pork slices. Repeat layers twice, adding some of the reserved liquid with each layer. Bake, uncovered, at 300 degrees for 5 to 6 hours, until beans are very tender. Add water as needed to keep beans covered. Makes 8 to 10 servings.

When measuring molasses, honey or other sticky ingredients, spray the measuring cup with non-stick vegetable spray first. The contents will slip right out and you'll get a more accurate measurement.

Grandma's Sunday Suppers

Beef Pasty Pie

Debbie Hunt
Wendell, ID

When time was short, my grandmother used to make this pie
instead of individual pasties. We liked pasties, either way!

2 10-inch pie crusts
3 to 4 potatoes, peeled and diced
1 lb. ground beef
1 onion, diced

1/2 c. catsup
3 T. Worcestershire sauce
salt and pepper to taste
Optional: beef gravy

Arrange one crust in a 10" pie plate; set aside. In a saucepan over medium heat, cover potatoes with water. Cook just until tender; drain. Meanwhile, in a skillet over medium heat, brown beef with onion. Drain; stir in catsup, Worcestershire sauce, salt and pepper. Add potatoes to beef mixture; spoon into pie crust. Cover with remaining pie crust; pinch edges to seal and make several slits in crust with a knife tip. Bake at 350 degrees for 30 minutes, or until bubbly and crust is golden. Cut into wedges. Serve hot or cold, topped with gravy, if desired. Makes 4 to 6 servings.

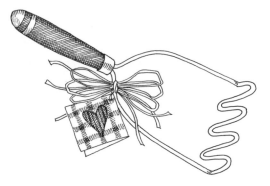

An easy way to crumble ground beef...use a potato masher.
It makes browning so quick & easy.

Mom's Spicy Cabbage Rolls

Sherry Svoboda
Bel Air, MD

This recipe takes me back to my childhood, when dinner was always centered around the family table...Mom, Dad, my brother and me, and the aroma of everyone's favorite meal. Serve with hot mashed potatoes and buttered soft French bread to dip in the tasty broth. I am now a grandmother of four and have passed this recipe on to my grown-up children.

1 head cabbage, cored
1-1/2 lbs. ground beef
1 onion, chopped
dried parsley, garlic salt,
    seasoning salt and pepper
    to taste
2 c. cooked rice

1 c. beef broth
28-oz. can whole peeled
    tomatoes, crushed
2 14-1/2 oz. cans diced
    tomatoes with zesty
    mild chiles

Drop cabbage into a large pot of boiling water; bring to a boil. Boil for several minutes; use tongs to remove 18 leaves as they soften. Line the bottom of an ungreased 13"x9" baking pan with 6 leaves; set aside remaining 12 large leaves. In a large skillet over medium heat, brown beef with onion. Drain; stir in seasonings and rice. Divide beef mixture into 12 portions. Spoon into the center of 12 large cabbage leaves. Fold in the sides of each leaf and roll up. Arrange cabbage rolls in pan. In a bowl, combine beef broth and crushed tomatoes with juice; spoon over cabbage rolls. Top with both cans of undrained diced tomatoes. Bake, covered, at 350 degrees for 1-1/2 hours, until hot, bubbly and cabbage rolls are tender. Makes 6 servings, 2 rolls each.

Love cabbage...but don't love the aroma? Use an old-fashioned trick to keep your house sweet-smelling. Just add a spoonful of vinegar, a lemon wedge or half an apple to the cooking pot.

Sausage Noodle Dinner

Christie Schenck
Somerset, PA

This recipe was given to me by a friend of my grandmother's at my bridal shower, more than 15 years ago. It quickly became a family favorite. Substitute a bag of coleslaw mix for the cabbage, if you need to save a little time.

1 lb. ground pork sausage
1 head cabbage, thinly sliced
1 onion, thinly sliced
1 carrot, peeled and shredded
2 t. chicken bouillon granules
1/4 c. boiling water

16-oz. container sour cream
3/4 t. salt
1/2 t. pepper
8-oz. pkg. egg noodles,
  uncooked
Optional: chopped fresh parsley

Brown sausage in a large skillet over medium heat; drain. Add cabbage, onion and carrot; mix well. Dissolve bouillon in boiling water; pour into skillet. Cover and cook over medium-high heat until vegetables are tender, about 10 to 15 minutes. If necessary, add a little additional water. While sausage mixture is simmering, cook noodles according to package directions; drain. Reduce heat under skillet to low. Stir in sour cream, salt and pepper; heat through. Gently fold in cooked noodles. Garnish with parsley, if desired. Serves 4 to 6.

The easiest-ever way to cook egg noodles...bring a big pot of water to a rolling boil, then add the noodles. Remove from heat, cover and let stand for 20 minutes, stirring twice. Perfect!

Baked Pork Spaghetti

Sarah Mehlenbeck
Riverton, IL

This was my grandmother's recipe that she handed down to my mom before I was born. I'm not a big fan of traditional spaghetti, but everyone who tries this dish loves it. It's my kids' favorite too... it's delish!

16-oz. pkg. spaghetti, uncooked	1/4 t. salt
1 lb. bacon, cubed	1/4 t. garlic pepper
1 onion, diced	1/4 t. pepper
1 lb. ham steak, cubed	2-1/2 to 3 c. tomato juice
10-3/4 oz. can tomato soup	2 c. shredded Cheddar cheese

Cook spaghetti according to package directions; drain. Meanwhile, in a skillet over medium heat, cook bacon with onion until bacon is crisp; do not drain. Add ham, tomato soup and seasonings to skillet; stir. Reduce heat to low; mix in cooked spaghetti. Transfer mixture to a greased 13"x9" deep baking pan. Pour in enough tomato juice to make the mixture saucy. Top with shredded cheese. Bake, uncovered, at 425 degrees until bubbly and cheese is melted, about 15 to 20 minutes. Makes 8 to 10 servings.

Casseroles spell comfort food, but what if the recipe is large and your family is small? Simple...just divide the casserole ingredients into two smaller pans and freeze one for later!

Grandma's Shepherd's Pie

Nicole Whitten
Alberta, Canada

My grandma and I used to make this tasty recipe often.
After she passed away, I continued to make it...it reminds me
of her and the time we had together.

8 to 10 potatoes, peeled
    and quartered
1 lb. ground beef
1 onion, diced
1 c. corn or mixed vegetables,
    drained

1 to 2 c. barbecue sauce
milk and butter to taste
2 c. shredded Colby Jack
    cheese

Cover potatoes with water in a large saucepan. Cook over medium-high heat until tender, 15 to 20 minutes. Meanwhile, brown beef in a skillet over medium heat. Add onion and cook until translucent; drain. Add corn or mixed vegetables; continue to cook for 5 minutes. Stir in barbecue sauce; cook for another 5 minutes. Drain potatoes; mash with milk and butter until smooth. Transfer beef mixture to a lightly greased 3-quart casserole dish. Spread mashed potatoes over beef mixture. Sprinkle cheese over potatoes. Bake, uncovered, at 350 degrees for 25 minutes, or until cheese is melted. Let stand for 5 minutes before serving. Make 8 servings.

Uncles and aunts, and cousins, are all very well,
and fathers and mothers are not to be despised;
but a grandmother...is worth them all.

– Fanny Fern

Skillet Meatloaf

Lauren Vanden Berg
Grandville, MI

My great-grandma was very poor and only owned one cast-iron skillet. She made this meatloaf in the skillet. She passed her skillet on to my grandma, who passed it on to me. Now this is the only kind of meatloaf I make.

1 lb. ground beef
1 onion, chopped
1 green pepper, chopped
4 saltine crackers, crushed

1-oz. pkg. ranch salad
   dressing mix
1 egg
1/4 c. barbecue sauce

In a bowl, combine beef, onion and green pepper; mix well. Add cracker crumbs and dressing mix; mix again. Shape beef mixture into a ball; make a little hole in the middle. Crack the egg into the hole; mix again. Preheat a cast-iron skillet over medium heat. Shape meatloaf to fit into skillet. Add meatloaf to skillet. Spread barbecue sauce on top. Cover skillet and cook for 20 to 25 minutes, until meatloaf is no longer pink in the center. Reduce heat to low, if needed. Serves 4.

Often, for the tastiest country cooking, no fancy tools
are needed. Dig right in and mix that meatloaf
with your hands!

Granny's Gravy Chicken

Diane Carter
Camden, TN

My mother-in-law Frances Rich Carter prepared this delicious chicken almost every Sunday when we all gathered at her house after church for lunch. I know she was making it in the 1960s and I think the addition of barbecue sauce was her idea. I now make it for my husband & myself. We always have creamed potatoes with it and use the extra gravy on them.

1-1/2 c. water
1/3 c. white vinegar
1 to 2 T. favorite barbecue sauce
1 t. salt
1 t. pepper
3/4 c. shortening, melted
3 to 3-1/2 lbs. chicken pieces
1-1/2 c. all-purpose flour

Combine all ingredients except chicken and flour in a deep 3-quart casserole dish. Mix well; bring to a boil in the oven at 350 degrees, or heat in the microwave. Meanwhile, place chicken in a large plastic zipping bag; add flour. Close bag and shake until well coated. Add chicken to boiling liquid. Sprinkle any extra flour from bag over chicken. Spoon hot liquid over flour until all moistened. If there is not enough liquid, add a little hot water. Bake, uncovered, at 350 degrees for one to 1-1/2 hours, turning chicken halfway through cooking time. Liquid and flour will turn into gravy. If gravy is getting too thick, add a little more hot water; stir to a smooth consistency. Makes 6 to 8 servings.

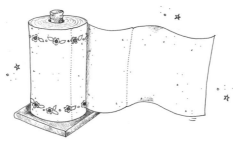

Old-fashioned recipes often start with, "Wash your chicken." This actually is no longer recommended...just pat chicken dry with a paper towel, if needed. However, after handling raw chicken, be sure to wash hands, countertops, cutting boards and knives with soapy hot water.

Chicken Schnitzel

Michelle Krumenacher
Richmond, IL

My German-Hungarian Oma was an amazing cook. She knew this was one of my favorites and would make it for me often. Now I make it for my family and it's a favorite with my boys, too.

1 lb. boneless, skinless chicken
    breasts
salt and pepper to taste
1 c. all-purpose flour

1 egg
1/2 c. milk
1 c. dry bread crumbs
1/2 c. oil

If chicken breasts are large, cut in half. Pound chicken with a kitchen mallet into 1/4-inch thick cutlets. Season with salt and pepper; set aside. Add flour to a shallow bowl or pie plate. Whisk egg and milk together in a separate bowl or plate; add bread crumbs to another. Dredge chicken cutlets in flour, shaking off any excess; dip in egg mixture, then coat with bread crumbs. Heat oil in a large skillet over medium heat until hot. Add chicken; cook until golden on the bottom. Flip and cook other side until golden and juices run clear. Drain on a paper towel-lined plate. Serves 4.

Keep a shaker canister of quick-mixing flour on hand for dredging meats before browning. It's terrific for making lump-free gravies too.

Gram's One-Pot Grub

Sandy Coffey
Cincinnati, OH

My kids and grandkids don't always eat vegetables, but they gobble down this dish, vegetables & all, and don't think twice! Add a basket of your favorite bread and enjoy.

2-lb. beef chuck roast
14-1/2 oz. can crinkle-cut
 carrots
14-1/2 oz. can sliced green
 beans
3 stalks celery, cut into
 2-inch pieces

4 to 5 potatoes, peeled
 and diced
1 onion, diced
1 green pepper, cut into strips
28-oz. container beef broth
salt and pepper to taste

Place roast in a Dutch oven with a lid. Around roast, add carrots and beans with their liquid; add remaining vegetables. Pour in beef broth; season with salt and pepper. Cover and bake at 325 degrees for 3-1/2 hours. Turn oven off; let stand in the oven for 30 minutes. Makes 4 to 5 servings.

A large roasting pan can handle plenty of kitchen tasks besides roasting chicken, turkey and pot roasts. It's also terrific for oven-browning batches of meatballs, stirring up lots of snack mix... even set it over 2 stovetop burners and boil sweet corn for a crowd!

Grandma's Sausage & Rice Casserole

Earleen Richeson
Taylorsville, KY

This recipe originated with my mother-in-law, who was a wonderful cook. Everyone always liked to eat dinner at her house. This casserole is different from any other casserole I have eaten, and it's excellent served with tossed salad and warm bread. Hope you enjoy it as much as my family does.

2 lbs. mild ground pork sausage
3/4 c. onion, diced
1 c. green pepper, diced
2-1/2 c. celery, diced
4-1/2 c. water

2 1-3/4 oz. pkgs. chicken
   noodle soup
1 c. instant rice, uncooked
1/2 t. salt

In a large skillet over medium heat, cook sausage, onion, green pepper and celery until sausage is no longer pink and vegetables are soft; drain. Meanwhile, in a large saucepan, bring water to a boil. Stir in soup mix, rice and salt; simmer over medium-low heat for 20 minutes. Add sausage mixture and mix well. Transfer to a lightly greased 12"x8" baking pan. Bake, uncovered, at 375 degrees for 20 minutes. Makes 8 to 10 servings.

Use Grandma's vintage baking dishes from the 1950s to serve up casseroles with sweet memories. If you don't have any of hers, keep an eye open at yard sales and thrift stores... you may find the very same kind of dishes she used!

Porky Pigs in a Blanket

Patricia Tiede
Cheektowaga, NY

*This was my German Gramma's recipe. I've never seen one
like it in print. My family loves it because it's a new twist
on the traditional stuffed cabbage recipes.*

1 head cabbage	1/8 t. nutmeg
2 c. cooked pork, cubed	salt and pepper to taste
1/3 c. dry bread crumbs	3 c. pork gravy, divided
1 T. onion, finely chopped	

Remove 8 to 12 leaves from outside of cabbage. Drop into boiling
water for 2 to 3 minutes, until softened; set aside. Grind or finely
chop remaining cabbage. Grind pork or chop finely in a food processor.
In a large bowl, combine pork, bread crumbs, 1/4 cup ground cabbage,
onion, seasonings and 2 tablespoons gravy. Mix thoroughly. Use
about 1/4 cup of pork mixture for each cabbage leaf. Form into an
egg shape; place on cabbage leaf and roll up. Place rolls in a lightly
greased 3-quart casserole dish, seam-side down. Pour remaining gravy
over top. Cover loosely with aluminum foil. Bake at 350 degrees for
30 minutes. Serves 4.

When making a favorite casserole, why not make a double batch?
After baking, let the extra casserole cool and tuck it in the freezer...
ready to share with a new mother, carry to a potluck or reheat
on a busy night at home.

Henny-Penny Chicken

Kathy Courington
Canton, GA

My mother had a fun name for every yummy casserole. She made this one often because it was so simple and she loved simple recipes.

2 c. cooked chicken, cubed
2 c. celery, diced
1 c. mayonnaise
2 T. lemon juice
1/2 c. toasted slivered almonds

1/2 t. salt
Optional: 1/2 t. flavor enhancer
1/2 c. potato chips, crushed
1/2 c. American cheese, grated

In a large bowl, combine all ingredients except potato chips and cheese; mix well. Transfer to a buttered 2-quart casserole dish. Top with chips and cheese. Bake, uncovered, at 400 degrees for 15 to 20 minutes, until heated through and cheese melts. Makes 4 to 6 servings.

Create a family recipe book of all the best handed-down favorites. Tuck a sweet photo in the front and tie it all up with a bow...a gift to be treasured.

Johnny Marzetti

Jennie Gist
Gooseberry Patch

An old midwestern favorite! My grandmother in northern Ohio used to make this hearty dish for my family whenever we came to visit.

1 lb. lean ground beef
2 onions, sliced
1 clove garlic, minced
1-1/2 c. water
6-oz. can tomato paste
1 t. vinegar
7-oz. can sliced mushrooms, drained

1 c. celery, diced
1 green pepper, diced
8-oz. pkg. sharp pasteurized process cheese spread, cubed
salt and pepper to taste
8-oz. pkg. elbow macaroni, uncooked

In a large skillet over medium heat, brown beef, onions and garlic. Drain; stir in water, tomato paste and vinegar. Add remaining ingredients except macaroni. Simmer over low heat, stirring occasionally, about 15 minutes. Meanwhile, cook macaroni according to package directions; drain and return to cooking pot. Stir in beef mixture. Cover and simmer over low heat until heated through, about 15 minutes. For a casserole-style dish, transfer beef and macaroni mixture to a greased 3-quart casserole dish. Bake, uncovered, at 350 degrees for 20 to 25 minutes, until hot and bubbly. Makes 6 to 8 servings.

If your favorite casserole tends to drip or bubble over in the oven, place a sheet of aluminum foil under the pan to catch drippings. Clean-up's a snap!

Polish Spaghetti

Lorraine Pollachek
Boca Raton, FL

My grandmother created this dish. She and my grandfather were first-generation American-born Polish. What else would we call it? Tip: this casserole can only be made with leftover pork. It just isn't the same with freshly cooked pork! Serve hot with a tossed salad or green vegetable.

16-oz. pkg. spaghetti, uncooked
   and broken in half
4 c. cooked pork, cut into
   3/4-inch cubes
1/4 c. oil
2 T. garlic powder
2 T. dried parsley

1 t. salt
1/2 t. pepper
2 10-3/4 oz. cans tomato soup
1 onion, diced
1-1/4 c. grated Parmesan
   cheese, divided

Cook spaghetti according to package directions; drain. Meanwhile, heat oil in a skillet over medium heat until just starting to brown. Add pork and seasonings; increase heat to medium-high. Cook just until pork starts to brown; drain. Place cooked spaghetti in a lightly greased 3-quart casserole dish. Add pork, soup, onion and one cup cheese; toss well. Top with remaining cheese. Bake, uncovered, at 375 degrees for about 30 minutes, until heated through and a crust begins to form on top. Makes 4 to 6 servings.

Keep a chunk of Parmesan cheese fresh longer. Simply wrap it in a paper towel that has been moistened with cider vinegar, tuck into a plastic zipping bag and refrigerate.

Grandma's Pork Chop Onion-Rice Bake

Georgia Muth
Penn Valley, CA

My grandma made these delicious pork chops as far back as I can remember. Her recipe dates back to the mid 1950s and is still a favorite in our family.

6 bone-in pork chops,
  1-inch thick
2 T. oil
1 c. long-grain rice, uncooked
1.35-oz. pkg. onion soup
  mix, divided

1/3 c. sliced mushrooms
Optional: 2 T. diced pimentos
3 c. hot water

In a large skillet over medium-high heat, brown pork chops in oil. Spread uncooked rice in a greased 13"x9" baking pan. Set aside one tablespoon soup mix. Sprinkle remaining soup mix over rice. Spread mushrooms and pimentos, if using, over rice. Pour the hot water over rice. Arrange browned chops on top. Sprinkle chops with reserved soup mix. Cover tightly with aluminum foil. Bake at 350 degrees until chops are tender, 45 minutes to one hour. Remove foil and cook 10 minutes longer, or until any excess liquid evaporates. Makes 6 servings.

When pork chops are on the menu, sprinkle a little salt in your cast-iron skillet before adding the oil and the chops. You'll have less spattering and more flavorful pork chops.

Aunt Ella Mae's Raised Doughnuts, page 25

Amazing Overnight Waffles, page 9

Peanut Butter Bread, page 46

Fruit Salsa Spread & Dip, page 176

Anna Mae's No-Fail Peach Cobbler, page 212

California Avocado Soup, page 34

Corn Fritters, page 64

Nana's Chicken à la King, page 49

Grandma Mitten's Oatmeal Cookies, page 183

Colby Corn Chowder, page 33

Really Good Guacamole, page 158

Johnny Marzetti, page 108

3-Bean Basil Salad, page 79

Grandma's Cucumbers, page 69

Grandma Ella's Chicken & Dumplings, page 126

Grandma's Tomato Muffins, page 54

Uncle Jesse's Ambrosia Salad, page 83

Speedy Spanish Rice, page 93

Skillet Cherry Pie, page 211

Grandma's Shepherd's Pie, page 100

Vegetable Beef Soup, page 34

Cream of Asparagus Soup, page 41

Grandma's Shortbreads, page 189

Pork Chop-Potato Scallop

Shirl Parsons
Cape Carteret, NC

This is a recipe from my husband's grandmother, Thelma Skelton. She was well known as a great cook.

1 lb. pork chops	1/4 c. water
1 T. oil	2 T. fresh parsley, chopped
10-3/4 oz. can cream of	4 c. potatoes, peeled and thinly
mushroom soup	sliced
1/2 c. sour cream	salt and pepper to taste

In a skillet over medium heat, brown pork chops in oil. Drain and remove chops to a plate; blend in soup, sour cream, water and parsley. In a lightly greased 2-quart casserole dish, layer potatoes with salt, pepper and sauce. Top with pork chops. Cover and bake at 350 degrees for one hour and 15 minutes. Serves 4.

Grandmom's Fancy Pork Chops

Megan Simpson
Smithsburg, MD

This recipe was created by my Grandmom and it was her favorite meal to make for family get-togethers. She always served this dish with mashed potatoes and green beans.

1 lb. boneless pork chops	1/4 c. brown sugar, packed
1 onion, thinly sliced and	15-oz. can tomato sauce
separated into rings	1 T. Worcestershire sauce

Place pork chops in a lightly greased 13"x9" glass baking pan. Layer onion rings over pork chops. Sprinkle brown sugar over all. Mix sauces together; pour over top. Cover dish tightly with aluminum foil. Bake at 350 degrees for one hour and 15 minutes. Serves 4.

Don't cry when you chop onions!
Place them in the freezer
for 5 minutes first.

Mama Mia! Heavenly Marinara Sauce *Ansley Nichols*
Marietta, GA

The scent of marinara sauce bubbling away on the stove instantly transports me back to my grandmother's kitchen as well as to my long-wished-for trip to Italy. A teaspoon of sugar brings out the natural sweetness of the tomatoes.

1 T. olive oil	1/2 t. dried basil
1 onion, chopped	1/2 t. dried oregano
1 to 2 cloves garlic, minced	3/4 t. salt
28-oz. can crushed tomatoes	1/8 t. pepper
3/4 c. water	cooked spaghetti
1 t. sugar	

Heat oil in a large saucepan over medium heat. Sauté onion and garlic, stirring frequently. Add remaining ingredients; stir well. Bring to a boil; reduce heat to low. Cover and simmer, stirring occasionally, for about 20 minutes. Serve sauce over spaghetti. Makes 10 to 12 servings.

Celebrate Grandparents' Day, September 12, by inviting Grandma & Grandpa to dinner. Let them take it easy while the rest of the family does all the cooking and serving!

Baked Eggplant Parmesan

Mia Rossi
Charlotte, NC

My grandma always made the best Eggplant Parmesan. I never got her recipe, though, so I was happy to find this recipe that's almost as good. I like to use the canned tomatoes and tomato sauce that come already seasoned with garlic, basil and oregano...a money saver that Grandma didn't have!

1/4 c. Italian-flavored dry bread crumbs
1/4 c. grated Parmesan cheese
1 to 2 eggplants, peeled if desired and cut into 12 slices, 1/2-inch thick
1/4 c. butter, melted

1 c. shredded mozzarella cheese
14-1/2 oz. can diced tomatoes
8-oz. can tomato sauce
Italian seasoning and garlic powder to taste
Optional: cooked spaghetti

Combine bread crumbs and Parmesan cheese in a shallow dish. Brush eggplant slices with melted butter; coat each side with bread crumb mixture. Arrange on a lightly greased baking sheet. Bake, uncovered, at 425 degrees for 15 minutes, or until tender, turning once. Sprinkle eggplant slices evenly with mozzarella cheese. Meanwhile, combine tomatoes with juice, tomato sauce and seasonings in a small saucepan. Bring to a boil over medium-high heat. Reduce heat to medium-low. Simmer 10 minutes, or until slightly thickened. To serve, divide sauce among 4 plates; top with eggplant slices. Serve with cooked spaghetti, if desired. Serves 4 to 6.

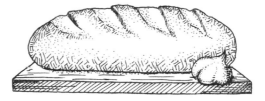

Pop some Parmesan bread in the oven while dinner is cooking.
Blend 1/4 cup butter, 2 tablespoons grated Parmesan cheese,
2 teaspoons minced garlic and 1/4 teaspoon Italian seasoning.
Spread it over a halved loaf of French bread and broil until golden.

Nana's Chicken à la King

Laurie Yanz
Webster, NY

*My grandchildren love this dish on a cold day after playing outside.
It is so easy they can help make it. They all wear their chef aprons
when we cook together. It is a wonderful sharing time for all of us.
I always double this recipe, because it goes very quickly!*

1/4 c. butter
1/3 c. all-purpose flour
1/2 t. salt
1 c. whole milk
1 c. chicken broth
10-3/4 oz. can cream of
   chicken soup

2 c. cooked chicken, diced
3-oz. can sliced mushrooms,
   drained
1/4 c. chopped pimentos, or
   more to taste
cooked noodles or rice,
   or baked biscuits

Melt butter in a large frying pan over medium heat. Add flour and salt;
stir together. Add milk and chicken broth all at once. Cook, stirring
constantly, over medium-high heat until sauce is thickened and
bubbly. Stir in soup, chicken, mushrooms and pimentos; heat through.
To serve, spoon over cooked noodles or rice, or split biscuits. Serves 4.

Serve old-fashioned creamed dishes in crisp toast cups. Trim crusts
from bread slices, spread both sides lightly with softened butter
and press gently into muffin cups. Bake at 350 degrees for
8 to 10 minutes, until toasted. Fill as desired.

Pressed Chicken

Pat Suey
Omaha, NE

My Grandma Mockelman was the best cook! We looked forward to special occasions and holidays when we knew she would make her delicious pressed chicken. We would slather butter on her homemade rye bread, top with pieces of pressed chicken and bite into a piece of heaven...mmm!

4 to 5-lb. chicken, cut up	1 to 2 bay leaves
1/2 c. onion, chopped	sliced rye or wheat bread
salt and pepper to taste	Garnish: softened butter

Place chicken in a stockpot; add just enough water to cover. Add onion and seasonings to pot. Bring to a boil over medium heat; reduce heat to medium-low. Simmer for 1-1/2 to 2 hours, until chicken is tender, adding more water as it cooks off. When chicken is tender, remove to a platter and let cool. Reserve broth in pot; discard bay leaves and skim off any fat. Remove chicken from bones; grind chicken in a meat grinder or food processor. Combine chicken in pot with just enough of reserved broth to moisten well. Divide chicken among 2 to 3 loaf pans, depending on pan size. Press down with a spoon, spooning off any excess broth. Cover loaf pans and refrigerate until chicken is firmly set. Loosen chicken in pans with a knife; turn out of pans. Slice thinly; serve in sandwiches on buttered bread. Keep any unused portion refrigerated. Makes 8 to 10 servings.

An old-fashioned food grinder is handy for grinding meat for spreads, meatloaf and other recipes. To clean it easily when you've finished, just put a half-slice of bread through the grinder. The bread will remove any food particles.

Grandmommy's Chicken Pie

Brenda Rogers
Atwood, CA

My grandmother called this casserole her Chicken Pie. Generations of my family have made and loved it. It is delicious hot from the oven. My kids always liked it leftover and cold from the fridge too!

10-3/4 oz. can cream of
    mushroom soup
1-1/4 c. milk
2 c. cooked chicken, chopped
1/2 c. onion, diced

2 c. pasteurized process cheese
    spread, grated
2 sleeves saltine crackers,
    crushed

In a bowl, whisk together soup and milk. In a greased 2-quart casserole dish, spread a little of the soup mixture in the bottom. Layer half each of chicken, onion, cheese and crackers; pour a little of remaining soup mixture over top. Continue layering; spread remaining soup mixture over top. Bake, uncovered, at 350 degrees for about 45 minutes, until bubbly and a little golden on top. Remove from oven; let stand for about 15 minutes. Makes 6 to 8 servings.

If your recipe call for cracker crumbs, first seal them in a
plastic zipping bag. A cereal box liner works great too.
Then crush with a rolling pin...no mess!

Chicken Stew

*Pamela Moss
Ann Arbor, MI*

I always loved it when my mom was making this stew...it has been simmering in my family for as long as I can remember! Until now, it hasn't been written down anywhere. Use fresh or canned veggies.

3-1/2 lbs. chicken
28-oz. can stewed tomatoes
14-3/4 oz. can creamed corn
15-1/4 oz. can corn, drained
14-1/2 oz. can green beans,
   drained
6-oz. can tomato paste
3 to 4 potatoes, peeled and
   cubed

1 to 2 onions, chopped
1/2 to 1 c. okra, sliced
1 stalk celery, chopped
salt and pepper to taste
Optional: red pepper flakes
   to taste
Garnish: shredded Cheddar
   cheese

In a large soup pot, cover chicken with water. Bring to a boil over medium heat. Reduce heat to medium-low; simmer until tender, about 1-1/2 hours. Remove chicken to a platter; strain and reserve 2 cups broth in pot. Pull chicken from bones when cool. Return chicken to reserved broth in pot; add tomatoes with juice and remaining ingredients except cheese. Simmer over medium heat until vegetables are tender, stirring often, 20 to 25 minutes. Serve in bowls, sprinkled with cheese. Makes 8 servings.

Don't let leftover chopped herbs go to waste! Spoon them into an ice cube tray, cover with water and freeze. Frozen cubes can be dropped right into simmering stews or vegetable dishes for an extra punch of flavor.

Mom's Tamale Pie

Joan Chance
Houston, TX

*My mom was ahead of her time. Instead of fixing the usual meat &
potato dishes, we learned to eat Tex-Mex before it was popular!
Before polenta, too...we knew it as cornmeal mush.*

5 c. water, divided
1 t. salt
1 c. cornmeal
2 T. butter
1/4 c. onion, chopped
1/2 c. green pepper, chopped
1 clove garlic, minced
1 lb. ground beef

1 T. all-purpose flour
2 t. chili powder, or more
   to taste
1/8 t. pepper
2-1/2 c. tomatoes, chopped
1/2 c. sliced black olives,
   drained

In a large saucepan over medium heat, bring 4 cups water to a boil;
add salt. In a bowl, mix cornmeal with remaining cold water; slowly
add to boiling water. Cook and stir over low heat until thickened,
about 15 minutes. Remove from heat; set aside. Melt butter in a large
skillet over medium heat; add onion, green pepper and garlic. Cook for
3 minutes. Set mixture aside in a bowl; brown beef in the same skillet,
until no longer pink. Return onion mixture to skillet along with
remaining ingredients; stir well. Spoon a thin layer of cooked cornmeal
into a lightly greased 2-quart casserole dish. Top with beef mixture;
spread remaining cornmeal on top in a thin layer. Bake, uncovered,
at 350 degrees for one hour, or until heated through and golden on
top. Makes 6 to 8 servings.

Keep a sturdy pair of kitchen scissors on hand. They make
quick work of snipping fresh herbs, chopping green onions
or even cutting up whole tomatoes right in the can.

Mexican Stuffed Shells

Kathy Courington
Canton, GA

*A friend of my mother's made this for us years ago. She kindly
shared the recipe with me. The cumin gives the meat a smoky
taste...it's a nice variation on the usual stuffed shells.*

12 jumbo pasta shells, uncooked
1 lb. ground beef
1 t. ground cumin
12-oz. jar medium or mild
    picante sauce
8-oz. can tomato sauce
1/2 c. water

4-oz. can chopped green chiles,
    drained
1 c. shredded Monterey Jack
    cheese, divided
6-oz. can French fried onions,
    divided
Optional: chopped fresh cilantro

Cook pasta shells according to package directions; drain. Meanwhile,
brown beef with cumin in a skillet over medium heat; drain. In a bowl,
combine sauces, water, chiles, 1/2 cup cheese and 1/2 can onions. Mix
well. Spread half of sauce mixture into a lightly greased 12"x8" baking
pan. Stuff shells with beef mixture; arrange seam-side down in pan.
Spoon remaining sauce over shells. Cover and bake at 350 degrees for
30 minutes. Uncover; top with remaining cheese and onions. Bake an
additional 5 minutes longer, until cheese is melted. Garnish with
cilantro, if desired. Makes 6 servings, 2 shells each.

No-mess stuffed shells! Instead of a spoon, use a pastry bag
to fill cooked pasta shells...better yet, use a plastic zipping
bag with one corner snipped off. They'll be filled in
no time and clean-up is a breeze.

Grandma Jean's Special Goulash
Wendy Lee Paffenroth
Pine Island, NY

My mother came up with this recipe back in the 1960s, originally making it on the stovetop. When she went back to work, she adapted it to the slow cooker. She said the lemon zest was the secret ingredient. It is always better the second day. so make a double batch! Serve with a crisp tossed salad and warm rolls.

2 to 3 lbs. stew beef cubes
2 to 3 T. oil
2 onions, quartered
2 to 3 c. water
14-oz. pkg. frozen sliced carrots, thawed
8-oz. can tomato sauce
1 T. paprika

1 t. lemon zest
1/4 t. dried marjoram
2 cubes beef bouillon
3 cloves garlic
Optional: pepper to taste
2 16-oz. cans whole peeled potatoes, drained

In a large skillet over medium heat, brown beef in hot oil. Remove beef with a slotted spoon to a 6-quart slow cooker. Add onions to remaining oil in skillet; cook until tender. Add onions to slow cooker, scraping up pan drippings with the onions. Add remaining ingredients except garlic and potatoes. Spear garlic cloves with wooden toothpicks; add to slow cooker. Cover and cook on high setting for 4 to 5 hours; add potatoes during last 2 hours. Discard garlic and toothpicks at serving time. Makes 6 servings.

No cowboy was ever faster on the draw than a grandparent
pulling a baby picture out of a wallet.

– Anonymous

Great Nana's Beer Roast

Cheryl Mason
Sugar Land, TX

I love keeping family recipes alive! This recipe comes from my husband's grandma. It's our son's favorite. It is also good made in a slow cooker. Serve the sauce over noodles...delicious!

3 to 4-lb. boneless beef
    chuck roast
salt and pepper to taste
1 onion, sliced

12-oz. can beer (not light beer)
1/3 c. chili sauce
3 T. brown sugar, packed
1 clove garlic, minced

Season roast with salt and pepper; place in a large roasting pan. Cover with onion slices. Combine remaining ingredients in a bowl; spoon over roast. Cover and bake at 350 degrees for 3-1/2 hours, basting occasionally with pan juices, until roast is tender. May also be prepared in a 6-quart slow cooker. Cover and cook on low setting for 6 to 8 hours, basting occasionally with cooking juices. Serves 6.

Browning adds savory flavor to a pot roast. Heat a cast-iron skillet or other heavy pan over medium-high heat for one to 2 minutes. Add oil and let warm. Add roast and cook on all sides, turning only occasionally, until roast is well browned.

Mom's German Roasted Pork Hocks & Sauerkraut

Karin Saunders
Ontario, Canada

An absolutely delicious and easy-to-make recipe from Germany.
My mom has made it since I was a child. The meat just falls off
the bones...so good! Wonderful served with mashed potatoes.

1 to 2 T. oil
8 pork hocks
1 onion, chopped

salt and pepper to taste
32-oz. jar sauerkraut, drained
    and rinsed

Coat the bottom of a large roasting pan with oil. Arrange pork hocks in pan; sprinkle with onion and season with salt and pepper. Bake, uncovered, at 400 degrees for 30 minutes to one hour, turning once to brown hocks on both sides. Add sauerkraut and enough water to cover hocks. Cover and bake for another 30 minutes, or until pork is tender. Serves 4 to 6.

Steam vegetables to keep their fresh-picked taste. Bring 1/2 inch water to a boil in a saucepan and add cut-up veggies. Cover and cook to desired tenderness, about 3 to 5 minutes. A quick toss with a little butter and they're ready to enjoy.

Bacon & Zucchini Goulash

Lori Peterson
Effingham, KS

*My Grandma Marge used to make this dish often for me when
I was little. It was my favorite and hers too! Every year now,
the first zucchini I pick in my garden is used for this recipe.*

6 to 8 thick slices bacon,
    cut into 1-inch pieces
1 to 2 zucchini, chopped
1/2 onion, chopped

2 cloves garlic, chopped
4 c. tomatoes, diced
1 c. elbow macaroni, uncooked
salt and pepper to taste

In a large skillet over medium heat, cook bacon with zucchini, onion
and garlic until vegetables are tender. Stir in tomatoes and uncooked
macaroni; season with salt and pepper. Bring to a boil; turn heat to
low and cover. Simmer for 20 to 30 minutes, until macaroni is tender
and juice is absorbed. Add a little water as macaroni simmers, if needed.
Makes 4 to 6 servings.

To show a child what once delighted you,
to find the child's delight added to your own,
this is happiness.

– J.B. Priestley

Hamburger Chop Suey

Joan Chance
Houston, TX

When I was growing up in Kansas, no one ate unusual recipes...
just the meat & potatoes plate. My mom made this dish regularly,
way before others did. I'm 81 and still enjoy it!

2 T. butter
1 onion, chopped
1 lb. ground beef
3 stalks celery, sliced
1/3 c. boiling water
1 cube beef bouillon
2-1/2 T. cornstarch
2 T. cold water

2 T. soy sauce
1/2 t. brown sugar, packed
1-1/2 t. salt
1/8 t. pepper
14-oz. can bean sprouts,
    drained
cooked rice or chow mein
    noodles

Melt butter in a skillet over medium heat; add onion and beef. Cook until beef is browned. Add celery, boiling water and bouillon cube. Cover and cook 5 minutes; stir well. In a small bowl, blend cornstarch, cold water, soy sauce, brown sugar and seasonings. Add to beef mixture; cook and stir until thickened. Add bean sprouts to skillet; heat through. Serve with cooked rice or chow mein noodles. Makes 4 to 6 servings.

Country cooks in Grandma's day were used to putting away fresh meat in large amounts for later use. Save money on meals... do as they did! At supermarket sales, stock up on on large packages of ground beef, chuck steak, chicken or pork chops. Repackage into recipe-size portions before freezing.

Grandma's
Sunday Suppers

Beef Sukiyaki

June Sabatinos
Salt Lake City, UT

My grandmother used to make this quick & easy dish. She used canned bamboo sprouts and mushrooms and it was delicious. Now I use fresh sprouts and mushrooms and it's even better.

1-1/2 lbs. beef skirt steak, partially frozen and thinly sliced
2 T. oil
1/2 c. low-sodium soy sauce
1/4 c. sugar

1 bunch green onions
1 c. sliced mushrooms
1 c. fresh bean sprouts
1 c. celery, chopped
cooked rice

In a skillet over medium heat, brown beef strips in oil. Add soy sauce and sugar; cook for about 3 minutes. Meanwhile, cut green part of onions into 1-1/2 inch lengths and set aside. Thinly slice white part of onions; add to beef mixture along with mushrooms, sprouts and celery. Cook until vegetables are crisp-tender. Add green part of onions; cook about one more minute. Serve with cooked rice. Makes 4 servings.

The secret to tender steamed rice! Cook long-cooking rice according to package directions. When it's done, remove the pan from heat, cover with a folded tea towel and put the lid back on. Let stand for 5 to 10 minutes, then fluff with a fork and serve.

Grandma Ella's Chicken & Dumplings
Amanda Davis
Evansville, IN

Our whole family absolutely loved it when my grandmother made her chicken & dumplings. We requested them for every family gathering because they were so delicious.

3-1/2 lb. whole chicken
2 c. water
32-oz. container chicken broth
2 24-oz. pkgs. frozen
    dumplings, uncooked

23-oz. can cream of chicken
    soup
salt and pepper to taste

Place chicken in a large stockpot; add enough water to cover chicken. Bring to a boil over medium heat; reduce heat to medium-low and cook until tender. Remove chicken to a platter and let cool. Reserve 3 to 4 cups broth in pot. Pull chicken off bones; chop or shred. To reserved broth, add 2 cups water and container of chicken broth. Bring to a boil over medium-high heat. Add frozen dumplings to boiling broth, one at a time, stirring after each dumpling is added. Add chicken and soup; stir well. Reduce heat to low. Simmer for about one hour, stirring occasionally, until dumplings are soft. Add salt and pepper to taste. Makes 10 to 12 servings.

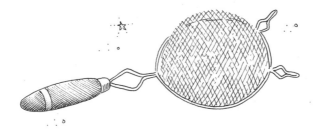

For the most flavorful chicken broth, start with bone-in chicken pieces and a cup or so of chopped onion, celery and carrot. A little garlic and parsley is good too. Cover with water and simmer gently until chicken is very tender, about one hour to 90 minutes. Strain broth through a mesh strainer.

Sunday Suppers

Sweet Onion Chicken

Vickie
Gooseberry Patch

This chicken is super-simple to fix and so flavorful. Serve with crusty bread to dip in the drippings...yum!

1/3 c. butter, melted
3-1/2 lbs. chicken
3 sweet onions, sliced
10 cloves garlic, chopped

1-1/2 t. salt
1/4 t. pepper
1/8 t. nutmeg

Spread melted butter in a 2-1/2 quart casserole dish. Add chicken pieces; turn to coat well with butter. Remove half of chicken and set aside. Arrange remaining chicken in casserole dish in a single layer. Top with half each of the onions, garlic and seasonings. Arrange remaining chicken on top; layer with remaining ingredients. Cover and bake at 375 degrees for 1-1/2 hours, or until chicken juices run clear when pierced. Makes 4 to 6 servings.

Sweet & Savory Chicken

Dale Duncan
Waterloo, IA

Gram's favorite quick recipe whenever we popped in for dinner.

3 T. Dijon mustard
2 T. apricot preserves
1 T. honey

1/2 t. ground ginger
4 boneless, skinless chicken
    breasts

In a bowl, combine all ingredients except chicken; mix well. Brush half of mustard mixture over chicken; reserve remaining mixture. Broil or grill chicken for 10 minutes per side, or until juices run clear, brushing with reserved mustard mixture. Serves 4.

A tasty apple coleslaw! Simply toss together a large bag of coleslaw mix, a diced Granny Smith apple, 1/2 cup mayonnaise and 1/2 cup plain Greek yogurt.

Braised Swiss Steak

Elizabeth Gallup
River Grove, IL

This is an easy, healthy recipe that my mom often made for our Sunday afternoon dinner. Delicious over buttered noodles or rice with a salad on the side.

2 T. dry bread crumbs
2 t. salt
1/4 t. pepper
2 lbs. beef round steak,
   1-inch thick
1 T. butter, melted

2 onions, thinly sliced
1/4 c. celery, chopped
1 T. Worcestershire sauce
1 clove garlic, crushed
8-oz. can stewed tomatoes
cooked noodles or rice

In a small bowl, combine bread crumbs, salt and pepper. Sprinkle half of crumb mixture on steak; pound into steak with a kitchen mallet. Repeat on other side of steak. Cut steak into 6 portions; set aside. Melt butter in a Dutch oven over medium heat. Add steak; brown well on both sides and remove from pan. Add onions, celery, Worcestershire sauce and garlic to pan drippings; bring to a boil. Reduce heat to low. Add steak and tomatoes with juice to pan. Cover and simmer for 2 hours, or until steak is tender. Serve steak portions over rice or buttered noodles. Serves 6.

Make mealtime extra special for your family. Even if no guests are coming for dinner, pull out the good china and light some candles...you'll be making memories together.

Mom's Spanish Steak

Joyce Borrill
Utica, NY

Easy and delicious...definitely a family favorite! Mom always said,
"The longer you let meat simmer, the more tender it will be."

1-1/2 to 2 lbs. beef round
   or sirloin steak, cut into
   serving-size portions
1-1/2 t. olive oil
2 to 3 green peppers, chopped

2 onions, sliced
14-oz. bottle catsup
1-3/4 c. water
1 clove garlic, pressed
salt and pepper to taste

In a Dutch oven or large skillet over medium-high heat, brown steak in olive oil. Drain; layer green peppers and onions over steak. Pour catsup over all. Add water to catsup bottle and shake; pour over all. Season with garlic, salt and pepper. Reduce heat to low. Cover and simmer for one to 3 hours, until steak is tender. Uncover during last 30 minutes to allow pan juices to thicken. Makes 6 servings.

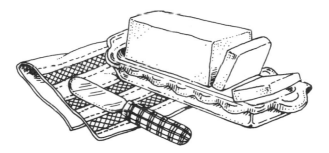

Add a little butter to the oil when sautéing...it helps foods
cook up golden and adds delicious flavor.

Mulligan Stew

Sandra Morgan
Navarre, FL

The smell of this stew cooking brings back such fond memories! My grandfather was a coal miner in Pennsylvania. He and my grandma had seven children. My grandma often made this recipe, as it was a great way to use up leftovers when things were tight. It pairs well with a grilled cheese sandwich or crusty French bread.

1 to 1-1/2 lb. ham steak, diced
   into bite-size chunks
3 to 4 potatoes, peeled and cut
   into bite-size chunks
1/2 c. onion, sliced
1 T. dried parsley

1 t. celery seed
2 to 3 c. water
2 14-1/2 oz. cans diced or
   stewed tomatoes
15-1/4 oz. can sweet peas,
   drained

In a Dutch oven, combine ham, potatoes, onion, parsley and celery seed. Cover just to top of mixture with water. Add tomatoes with juice. Simmer over medium-high heat, stirring occasionally, until potatoes are tender, about 15 to 20 minutes. Just before serving stir in peas; warm through. Serves 6 to 8.

For a zippy lemon salad dressing, shake up 1/2 cup olive oil,
1/3 cup fresh lemon juice and a tablespoon of Dijon mustard in
a small jar and chill to blend.

Grandma's Goulash

Valerie Bigham
Kendall, WI

*All of us grandkids loved Grandma Pauline's goulash. It's simple and
a little on the sweet side. Some of us like to add kidney beans or
crispy bacon. May also use bacon-flavored western dressing.*

16-oz. pkg. elbow macaroni,
   uncooked
1 lb. ground beef
1 onion, diced

salt and pepper to taste
2 c. catsup
2 c. western salad dressing

Cook macaroni according to package directions; drain. Meanwhile, in
a large skillet over medium heat, brown beef with onion. Drain; season
with salt and pepper. Add cooked macaroni to beef mixture. Add catsup
and salad dressing; mix well. Add more catsup or salad dressing, if
desired. Pour into a lightly greased 2-quart casserole dish. Bake at
350 degrees for 20 to 30 minutes, until hot and bubbly. Serves 4 to 6.

When pasta will be put into a baked casserole, cook the pasta
for the shortest cooking time recommended on the package.
It's not necessary to rinse the cooked pasta, just drain well.

Mallie Cat's Meatballs

Judy Taylor
Butler, MO

I don't remember how my granddaughter Mallory received the nickname "Mallie Cat", but these are her favorite meatballs. She always tells me "Grandma, I love your meatballs!" The sauce mixture also makes great baked beans. Sometimes I make extra sauce, as it can be kept refrigerated for a few days. Drain canned pork & beans, add to sauce and bake.

3 lbs. lean ground beef
12-oz. can evaporated milk
1 egg, beaten
1-1/2 c. quick-cooking oats,
    uncooked

1/4 c. onion, minced
2 t. chili powder
1/2 t. garlic powder
1-1/2 t. salt
1/2 t. pepper

In a large bowl, combine all ingredients. Mix well and shape into walnut-size balls. Arrange meatballs in a single layer in an ungreased 13"x9" baking pan. Spoon Special Sauce over meatballs. Bake, uncovered, at 350 degrees for one hour. Drain before serving. Makes 8 to 10 servings.

Special Sauce:

2 c. catsup
1-1/2 c. brown sugar, packed
1/4 c. onion, chopped

2 T. smoke-flavored cooking
    sauce
1/2 t. garlic powder

Combine all ingredients in a saucepan. Cook and stir over medium-low heat, until brown sugar is dissolved.

If it's been too long since you've visited with good friends, why not host a casual get-together? Potlucks are so easy to plan...everyone brings along their favorite dish to share. It's all about food, fun and fellowship!

Momma Jewell's Applesauce Meatloaf *Patricia Parker*
Cabool, MO

My mother was the head cook at a nursing home for many years. She would multiply recipes up to feed a hundred people. This is one of the favorites she made for the residents at the nursing home, and for her family too.

2 lbs. ground beef
1 egg, beaten
3/4 c. applesauce
1 c. dry bread crumbs
1 c. whole milk

1 t. salt
pepper to taste
1/2 c. catsup
3 T. brown sugar, packed
1 T. mustard

In a large bowl, combine beef, egg, applesauce, bread crumbs, milk, salt and pepper. Mix well; shape into a loaf. Place in an ungreased 13"x9" baking pan. In a separate bowl, combine remaining ingredients; spread over meatloaf. Bake, uncovered, at 350 degrees for one hour. Makes 8 to 10 servings.

For a lower-fat meatloaf, simply pat the meat mixture into
a loaf shape and place it on a rimmed baking sheet.
Any excess fat will run off as the meatloaf bakes.

Bootsie's Macaroni & Cheese

Bootsie Dominick
Sandy Springs, GA

This has been a favorite with my five grandchildren. The oldest is 19 years old and in college; I have made it and sent it back to school with him. My tip for you: for the best flavor, shred your own cheese.

2 c. elbow macaroni, uncooked
2 eggs, beaten
1 c. milk
2 c. shredded sharp Cheddar
   cheese

1 c. small-curd cottage cheese
1/2 t. salt
1 c. shredded Monterey Jack
   cheese

Cook macaroni according to package directions; drain. Combine eggs, milk, Cheddar cheese, cottage cheese and salt. Add cooked macaroni; transfer to a greased 2-quart casserole dish. Top with Monterey Jack cheese. Bake, uncovered, at 350 degrees for 45 minutes to one hour. Makes 8 servings.

Grandma Lutz's Mac & Cheese

Krysti Hilfiger
Covington, PA

Gram's macaroni & cheese never tasted like anyone else's. No one could make it like her! For years I tried to make it myself. One day she let me in on a secret...it had an egg in it! Now all grown up with a family of my own, I make her mac & cheese for them. My husband says it the best he's ever had, even better than his own grandma's, which is quite the compliment!

1-1/2 c. cooked elbow macaroni
1 c. shredded sharp Cheddar
   cheese

1/2 c. milk
1 egg, lightly beaten
1 T. butter, diced

In a greased one-quart casserole dish, combine cooked macaroni, cheese, milk and egg; mix well. Dot with butter. Bake, uncovered, at 350 degrees for 30 to 35 minutes. Serves 2.

Edith's Lazy Man Spaghetti

Tammy Pickering
Fairport, NY

My grandmother taught me how to make this recipe over 25 years ago. She made it when things were tough and she had six mouths to feed. It probably should be called Busy Woman Spaghetti instead! She used tomatoes fresh-picked right out of her garden.

32-oz. pkg. spaghetti, uncooked
2 T. butter
1 lb. bacon, cut into bite-size
   pieces

2 14-1/2 oz. cans diced
   tomatoes
1 c. onion, chopped
2 t. salt

Cook spaghetti according to package directions, just until tender; drain. Transfer spaghetti to a lightly greased 3-quart casserole dish. Stir in tomatoes with juice and set aside. Melt butter in a skillet over medium heat. Add bacon and onion; cook until bacon is partially crisp and onion is tender. Drain; mix into spaghetti. Season with salt; mix well. Bake, uncovered, at 375 degrees for 20 minutes. Makes 8 servings.

Hosting a big family dinner? Ask everyone to bring a baby picture.
Have a contest...the first person to guess who's who gets a prize!

French-Fried Tomato Sandwiches

Jody Somogyi
Allentown, PA

You've never tasted anything like these yummy sandwiches before!
The recipe was handed down from my grandmother.

1/2 c. sour cream
1/2 c. Gruyère cheese, grated
2 T. fresh dill, snipped
2 T. fresh chives, snipped
lemon juice to taste
salt and white pepper to taste
3 T. butter, softened and divided

8 slices white or wheat bread,
  crusts trimmed
2 ripe tomatoes, sliced 1/4-inch
  thick
2 eggs
1/4 c. milk

In a bowl, combine sour cream, cheese and herbs. Season with lemon juice, salt and pepper; set aside. Using half of butter, spread butter on one side of each bread slice. Spread sour cream mixture on the buttered side of 4 slices, leaving a 1/4-inch border. Place a slice of tomato on each slice of buttered bread. Arrange remaining bread slices on the tomatoes, butter-side down. Press sandwiches together slightly. In a shallow dish, beat eggs and milk together; season with more salt and pepper. Melt remaining butter in a large heavy skillet over medium heat. Dip both sides of each sandwich into milk mixture; allow sandwiches to soak up milk mixture for a few seconds before transferring them to skillet. Cook sandwiches for 2 to 3 minutes on each side, until crisp and golden. Drain sandwiches on paper towels; cut into quarters and serve. Makes 4 servings.

Make grilled cheese sandwiches extra special...
grill 'em in a waffle iron!

Granny's Bubble Pizza

Jenny Bishoff
Mountain Lake Park, MD

This is a recipe from my grandmother. Once she took my toddler daughter and me on a trip to a nearby resort. Our accommodations had a complete kitchen, so she and I spent a day going through her recipes and planning our meals together...such fun! This is one she shared with me as a favorite when her boys were young.

3 7-1/2 oz. tubes refrigerated
   biscuits, quartered
8-oz. pkg. sliced pepperoni,
   quartered, or mini pepperoni
15-oz. jar pizza sauce

2 c. shredded mozzarella cheese
Optional: Italian seasoning
   and grated Parmesan cheese
   to taste

Spray a 13"x9" baking pan with non-stick vegetable spray. Scatter biscuit and pepperoni pieces in pan. Top with pizza sauce. Bake, uncovered, at 350 degrees for 25 minutes. Sprinkle with mozzarella cheese; add Italian seasoning and Parmesan cheese, if using. Bake 5 more minutes, or until cheese melts. Serves 6 to 8.

Set a regular dinner theme for each night of the week...
Spaghetti Night, Casserole Night or Pizza Night, based on
your family's favorites. You'll be creating memories
together, and meal planning is a snap!

Sunday Roast Chicken

Stephanie Mayer
Portsmouth, VA

There's nothing like chicken for Sunday dinner at Grandma's!
This recipe with delicious gravy is worth every step.

5 to 6-lb. roasting chicken
1 lemon
2 T. olive oil

3 T. fresh thyme, minced
5 cloves garlic, chopped
salt and pepper to taste

Place chicken in a roasting pan; set aside. Grate 2 teaspoons zest from lemon; cut lemon in quarters and place inside chicken. In a cup, combine lemon zest, olive oil, thyme and garlic; set aside one tablespoon of mixture for Pan Gravy. Rub remaining oil mixture over chicken. Season with salt and pepper. Tie legs of chicken with kitchen twine. Bake at 450 degrees for 20 minutes; turn oven to 375 degrees. Bake for about one hour and 15 minutes, until a meat thermometer inserted into thickest part of leg reads 170 degrees. Allow juices inside chicken to run into pan; transfer chicken to a serving platter. Cover lightly with aluminum foil while making Pan Gravy. Carve chicken and serve with Pan Gravy. Serves 6 to 8.

Pan Gravy:

juices from roasting pan
1/4 c. dry white wine or
   chicken broth

1 c. chicken broth
2 t. all-purpose flour
salt and pepper to taste

Pour pan juices into a large glass measuring cup; skim fat. Add wine or 1/4 cup broth to pan; place on stovetop over high heat. Bring to a boil; scrape up any browned bits. Pour hot mixture into cup with pan juices; set aside pan. Add enough broth to cup to measure 1-1/2 cups. Return broth mixture to pan. Stir flour into reserved oil mixture; whisk into broth mixture. On stovetop, cook and stir over medium heat for 2 minutes, or until slightly thickened. Season with salt and pepper.

Grandma's Chicken Pasties

Carrie Gering
Madisonville, TN

Back in the day, my Grandpa worked in a limestone quarry in Indiana. Before the sun was up, Grandma was up making breakfast for the family. She'd make these for Grandpa's lunch bucket too. Simple and simply delicious! Now we eat these on cold days (or not!) when we want something that'll stick to the ribs and bring back that homestyle feeling. P.S. It's pronounced PASS-ties!

2 c. cooked chicken, cubed	1 T. chopped pimentos, drained
3-oz. pkg. cream cheese, softened	1/4 t. salt
	1/8 t. pepper
6 to 7 T. butter, melted and divided	8-oz. tube refrigerated crescent rolls
2 T. milk	1/2 c. dry bread crumbs or
1 T. onion, minced	crushed croutons

In a bowl, combine chicken, cream cheese, 3 tablespoons melted butter, milk, onion, pimentos and seasonings. Mix well; mixture should be creamy but not thin. Unroll crescent roll dough. Separate dough into 4 squares; gently press together to seal seam. Spoon 1/2 cup of chicken mixture into the center of each square. Pull in all 4 corners, matching opposite corners diagonally; press gently to seal. Brush tops with remaining melted butter; cover with crumbs. Place pasties on an ungreased baking sheet. Bake at 350 degrees for 25 to 30 minutes, until lightly golden. Serve hot. Makes 4 to 6 servings.

Keep a ball of kitchen string right where you need it! Simply drop it into a small teapot and pull out the end of the string through the spout.

Calico Beans

Blanche DeLay
Kamiah, ID

My mother used to make this recipe. It was always a hit with our family...perfect for get-togethers! Now I make it for my family too. If you like, chopped ham can be used instead of bacon.

1/2 lb. bacon, chopped
3/4 c. onion, chopped
2 lbs. ground beef
1/2 c. catsup
1/2 c. brown sugar, packed
2 T. vinegar
1T. mustard

1 t. salt
15-3/4 oz. can pork & beans, drained
14-1/2 oz. can lima beans, drained
15-1/2 oz. can red kidney beans, drained

In a large skillet over medium heat, cook bacon and onion until bacon is crisp. Add beef; cook until no longer pink but not browned. Drain; transfer to a lightly greased 2-quart casserole dish. Add remaining ingredients; mix well. Bake, uncovered, at 300 degrees for 1-1/2 hours. Makes 8 servings.

Grandma believed in always having a full pantry...so should you!
With dried beans, pasta, rice, condiments, canned soups and veggies
in the cupboard you're all set to stir up a satisfying meal anytime.

Barbecued Hamburg Buns

Sara Wright
Colorado Springs, CO

My husband found this recipe in my grandmother's recipes. We really enjoy the flavors. It's special to have not only her original recipe but the little note my grandfather wrote on it: "Hi, Dreamboat!"

2 lbs. ground beef
1/2 c. onion, finely chopped
1 to 2 cloves garlic, minced
15-oz. can tomato sauce
1/2 c. catsup

1 T. sugar
1 T vinegar
1 T. mustard
8 hamburger buns, split

In a large skillet over medium heat, brown beef with onion and garlic. Drain. Meanwhile, in a saucepan over medium heat, combine remaining ingredients except buns. Stir well and bring to a boil; pour over beef mixture. Simmer until blended well. To serve, spoon beef mixture onto buns. Serves 8.

Set a Lazy Susan on the dinner table. So handy for everyone to reach the sauces and condiments they like...just give it a spin!

141

Grandma Astrid's Swedish Meatballs

Barbara Southern
Delavan, WI

My grandma always made these meatballs at Christmas time and then my mom carried on the tradition. They're delicious!

1/2 c. onion, chopped
3 T. butter, divided
1-1/2 lbs. ground beef,
    or 1 lb. ground beef plus
      1/2 lb. ground pork
1 c. light cream
1 egg, beaten
1-1/2 c. soft bread crumbs

1/4 c. fresh parsley, finely
    chopped, or 2 T. dried
    parsley
1/8 t. ground ginger
1/8 t. nutmeg
1-1/4 t. salt
1/8 t. pepper

In a skillet over medium heat, cook onion in one tablespoon butter until tender. Transfer onion mixture to a large bowl. Add beef and remaining ingredients. Mix well by hand. Moisten hands with water; shape into one-inch balls. Melt remaining butter in skillet over medium heat. Add meatballs and cook on all sides, until lightly browned and no longer pink in the center. Add a little more butter to skillet, if needed. Meatballs may be kept warm in a baking pan at 250 degrees. Makes about 40 meatballs.

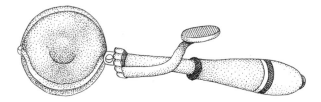

An old-fashioned ice cream scoop is handy for more than just serving up frozen treats. Use it to scoop muffin batter, mashed potatoes and even jumbo meatballs...perfect portions every time!

Ground Beef & Noodles Casserole

Judy Lange
Imperial, PA

A quick and inexpensive family dinner that we all enjoyed.
Add a loaf of fresh-baked homemade bread...so satisfying!

16-oz. pkg. broad egg noodles,
   uncooked
1 lb. ground beef
1/2 t. onion, minced
10-3/4 oz. can cream of
   mushroom soup

1/2 t. salt
1/2 t. pepper
1/2 c. soft bread crumbs
1 T. butter, melted

Cook egg noodles according to package directions; drain. Meanwhile, brown beef and onion in a skillet over medium heat; drain. Add cooked egg noodles, soup, salt and pepper. Mix well; transfer to a buttered 2-quart casserole dish. Combine bread crumbs and melted butter; spread over top. Bake, uncovered, at 350 degrees for 30 minutes, or until heated through. Serves 6 to 8.

Savor a beautiful evening by carrying dinner to the backyard... invite the next-door neighbors too! Kids can work up an appetite playing hide & seek or tag before dinner. Top off the evening with a super-simple dessert like frozen fruit pops in warm weather or marshmallows toasted over a fire ring in cool weather.

Cabbage Burgers

Jodi Icopini
Billings, MT

My mother & grandmother always made these filled sandwiches while I was growing up. I've made a few changes to suit my family's taste, and they continue to be a favorite we enjoy often.

1 env. active dry yeast
2 t. sugar
1/4 c. warm water, 110 to
    115 degrees
3/4 c. milk

1/2 t. salt
1 T. shortening, melted
2 c. all-purpose flour
Garnish: melted butter

In a large bowl, add yeast and sugar to warm water. Let stand 5 minutes, or until foamy. Heat milk almost to boiling; cool. Add milk, salt and shortening to yeast mixture; stir well. Add flour. Mix well until dough forms, adding a little more flour if needed. Knead dough on a floured surface until firm, smooth and elastic but not sticky. Place dough in a greased bowl; cover with a tea towel. Let rise until double, about 30 minutes. Meanwhile, make Beef Filling; set aside to cool. Roll out dough on a floured surface into a rectangle, 1/4-inch thick. Cut dough into 8, 5-inch squares. Place 2 heaping tablespoonfuls Beef Filling in the center of each square. Bring all 4 corners together and tightly pinch shut. Place filled squares, seam-side down, on a greased baking sheet. Let rise in a warm place for about 20 minutes. Bake at 375 degrees for 30 minutes, or until golden. Brush tops with melted butter. Serves 8.

Beef Filling:

1 lb. ground beef
3 c. cabbage, chopped
1-1/2 c. water

2 T. onion soup mix
1/2 t. seasoning
salt pepper to taste

In a skillet over medium heat, brown beef lightly; drain. Blend in remaining ingredients. Bring to a boil; reduce heat to low. Simmer, uncovered, for 20 minutes, or until all water has evaporated. Cool.

Unsure if your yeast is still good? Place one teaspoon yeast into one cup very warm water; add one tablespoon of sugar. If it foams and rises in 10 minutes, go ahead and use it.

Grandma's Best
Party Platters

Hawaiian Bowl Dip

Sherry Hill
Sylacauga, AL

My grandmother and I made this hot dip when I was in my teen years and I have been making it ever since. My family really enjoys it in the cool fall months, just in time for football. It is delicious and easy to make...everyone enjoys it.

16-oz. loaf Hawaiian sweet bread
8-oz. pkg. cream cheese, softened
12-oz. container sour cream
2 c. shredded sharp Cheddar cheese
2 c. shredded mild Cheddar cheese
1 bunch green onions, chopped
2-oz. pkg. deli honey ham, chopped
scoop-type corn chips

Leave bread in its aluminum foil pan. Cut off the top of bread and reserve. Scoop out the inside to make a bowl; set aside. In a bowl, blend cream cheese and sour cream. Fold in remaining ingredients except corn chips. Spoon mixture into hollowed-out bread; replace bread top. Wrap bread completely in foil. Bake at 350 degrees for one hour. Just before serving, remove bread top and stir dip very well. Serve with corn chips. Serves 8 to 10.

Pick up a dozen pint-size Mason jars...they're fun and practical for serving ice-cold lemonade, sweet tea or frosty root beer!

Spiced Pineapple Picks

Laurie Rupsis
Aiken, SC

*I got this recipe from my mother and I love it! It is just
a little bit different...a real treat at potlucks and parties.*

20-oz. can pineapple chunks
8-oz. can pineapple chunks
1-1/4 c. sugar

1/2 c. cider vinegar
4-inch cinnamon stick
8 whole cloves

In a saucepan, combine juice from both cans of pineapple chunks. Add
sugar, vinegar and spices; bring to a boil over medium heat. Reduce
heat to medium-low. Cover and simmer for 10 minutes. Add pineapple
chunks; return to a boil. Cook, stirring constantly, until heated
through. Serve pineapple chunks with toothpicks. Makes 12 servings.

Make a delicious party buffet even more inviting!
Arrange inverted cake pans or bowls on the table to
create different levels. Cover all with a tablecloth
and set food platters on top.

Gram's Chicken Dip

Linda McWilliams
Indian Trail, NC

This recipe has been a family favorite for over 50 years. My children's great-grandmother always made it during the holidays. It is a favorite and so easy to whip up at a moment's notice! I like to double the recipe for get-togethers. Yum!

8-oz. pkg. cream cheese,
   softened
4-1/4 oz. can white meat
   chicken spread

1/2 c. celery, diced
1/2 c. onion, diced
1/4 c. dry bread crumbs
shredded wheat crackers

In a bowl, mix together all ingredients except bread crumbs and crackers. Form into a half-dome on a plate. Sprinkle with bread crumbs; pat bread crumbs into place. Serve with crackers. Serves 4.

Southern Caviar

Dawn Timbs
Cord, AR

The quick dish we turn to for family entertaining! The southern gals in my family love their pimento cheese and my grandma is always looking for ways to change it up a bit. A jar of this spread is wonderful as a gift, tucked in a basket with some crackers.

14-oz. container pimento
   cheese spread
1 c. chopped pecans

1/2 c. dill pickle relish,
   or 1/4 c. sweet pickle relish
snack crackers

Combine all ingredients except crackers; blend well. Cover and chill overnight before serving. Serve with crackers. Serves 8.

A silver-plated baby spoon is ideal for serving up dollops
of a special party dip or condiment.

Dad's Beef & Chive Dip

Dacia Kennedy
Valley Center, KS

This is my version of a dip brought to family gatherings by my dad and my sister-in-law. Dad would purchase a favorite chip dip at the store, while my sister-in-law prepared her dip using a family recipe. I came up with this version by combining her recipe, my dad's recollection of the ingredients in the store brand and some changes of my own. Dad has been gone for 15 years now, but this dip can still be found at every family gathering.

2 8-oz. pkgs. cream cheese,
   softened
16-oz. container sour cream
16-oz. container sour cream &
   chive dip
5-oz. jar dried beef, cut into
   small squares

1/4 to 1/2 c. green onion,
   chopped
8-oz. pkg. shredded mild
   Cheddar cheese
snack crackers or bagel chips

In a serving bowl, combine cream cheese, sour cream and dip; blend well. Stir in beef, onion and shredded cheese. Cover and refrigerate at least one hour, until set. For a cheese ball variation, mix together all ingredients except Cheddar cheese and crackers or chips. Form mixture into a ball; roll in Cheddar cheese. Wrap ball in plastic wrap; chill overnight, until firm. Serve with crackers or bagel chips. Serves 24.

Colorful, fresh veggies are always welcome at parties and easy to prepare in advance. Cut them into bite-size slices, flowerets or cubes and tuck away in plastic zipping bags until needed. What a time-saver!

Pizza Cups

Carolyn Deckard
Bedford, IN

I started making these easy pizza cups for my first grandkid when she was four years old. That's 25 years ago. Now eight more grandkids and I am still making them! It's a quick treat they all like.

3/4 lb. ground beef
8-oz. can tomato sauce
1 T. onion, minced
1 t. Italian seasoning
1/2 t. salt
1/2 c. shredded mozzarella
    cheese
10-oz. tube refrigerated biscuits

In a large skillet over medium heat, cook beef until browned, stirring to crumble. Drain; stir in tomato sauce, onion and seasonings. Cook over medium heat for 5 minutes, stirring often. Place each biscuit in a greased muffin cup; press to cover bottom and sides. Spoon beef mixture into cups; sprinkle with cheese. Bake at 400 degrees for 10 to 12 minutes, until biscuits are golden. Serve warm. Makes 10 servings.

A quick and tasty appetizer trick that Grandma probably knew! Place a block of cream cheese on a serving plate, spoon sweet-hot pepper jelly over it and serve with crunchy crackers.

Filled Cheese Puffs

JoAnn
Gooseberry Patch

These mini cream puffs are perfect for a ladies' luncheon. Spoon in
your favorite filling like finely chopped chicken or shrimp salad.
Delicious and so pretty on a party table.

1 c. water
3 T. butter, sliced
3/4 t. salt
1/2 t. pepper
1 c. all-purpose flour

4 eggs
1/2 c. Gruyère cheese, finely
   shredded
1 c. favorite filling

In a saucepan, combine water, butter, salt and pepper. Bring to a boil
over medium-high heat. Add flour; stir with a wooden spoon until
dough forms. Transfer dough to a large bowl. In a separate bowl with
an electric mixer on high speed, beat eggs, adding one at a time,
beating well after each. Beat until smooth and cooled; beat in cheese.
Drop batter by tablespoonfuls, one-inch apart, onto buttered baking
sheets. With moistened fingers, smooth tops. Bake at 400 degrees for
25 to 30 minutes, until puffed and golden. Place baking sheets on wire
racks until puffs are cool. Slice off top 1/3 of each puff; pull out the
doughy centers. Spoon in filling; replace tops of puffs. Serves 8.

Primitive-style wooden cutting boards in fun shapes like pigs,
fish or roosters can often be found at tag sales. Put them
to use as whimsical party snack servers.

Ed's Cheese & Olive Balls

Gladys Kielar
Whitehouse, OH

Surprise family & friends with a new appetizer! These are always made by Papa Ed and shared at family get-togethers.

2 c. shredded sharp Cheddar
   cheese
1/2 c. butter, softened
1 c. all-purpose flour

1 t. paprika
1/2 t. salt
1/8 t. cayenne pepper
48 green olives with pimentos

In a bowl, blend cheese and butter. Stir in flour and seasonings; mix well. Wrap one teaspoon cheese mixture around each olive, covering completely. Arrange wrapped olives on a baking sheet; chill or freeze until firm. Bake at 375 degrees for 15 to 18 minutes, until golden. Serve warm. Makes 4 dozen.

George's Garlic Olives

Julie Brichetto-Thompson
Oakdale, CA

This recipe is from my Italian father George. People can never seem to get enough of these! You can serve them by themselves or as a side with dinner. Mangia!

15-oz. can jumbo or large black
   olives, drained and rinsed
2 to 3 T. extra-virgin olive oil

2 T. fresh Italian parsley,
   chopped
1 to 2 cloves garlic, pressed

Place olives in a paper towel-lined bowl. Drain for 5 minutes; discard towels. Add remaining ingredients; toss well. Cover and chill up to 8 hours before serving. For the best flavor, don't store overnight, as the garlic may become much stronger. Serves 4 to 6.

Serving appetizers before dinner?
Offer small bites like marinated
olives that will sharpen guests'
appetites but not fill them up.

Beef-Wrapped Pickles & Onions

Amy Lester
Roland, IA

My grandma and mom used to make these at the holidays. It was always a mad dash to see who would get to them first.

24-oz. jar baby dill pickles,
   drained
8 to 10 thin green onions,
   both ends cut off

35 to 40 thin slices dried beef
8-oz. container whipped cream
   cheese

Lay pickles on a paper towel to dry. Pat trimmed ends of onions dry. Spread each slice of dried beef evenly with cream cheese; top with a pickle or onion and roll up. Keep refrigerated. Serves 10.

Put out the welcome mat and invite friends over for a retro-style appetizer party. Serve up yummy finger foods from Grandma's day and play favorite tunes from the 1950s or 1960s. Everyone is sure to have a blast!

Annette's Cocktail Wieners

Diane LaBounty
Lyndonville, VT

My husband's mother Annette served these slow-cooked wieners at every family get-together. Even though she is no longer with us, we still look forward to her recipe at every family gathering. These will go fast...you may want to double the recipe!

1/2 c. catsup
1/2 c. chili sauce
2 T. brown sugar, packed
2 T. soy sauce
1/2 t. dried oregano

1/2 t. dry mustard
1/2 t. salt
1/4 t. pepper
1 lb. hot dogs, cut into
    bite-size pieces

In a 3-quart slow cooker, combine all ingredients except hot dogs. Stir well; add hot dogs and stir to coat. Cover and cook on low setting for 4 to 5 hours. Serves 6.

For a fun change from paper plates, pick up a stack of deli-style plastic baskets. Lined with crisp paper napkins, they'll hold each guest's heaping helping of appetizers with no spills.

154

Time-Out Chicken Wings

Darrell Lawry
Kissimmee, FL

An oldie but goodie that I just rediscovered...it's too good to forget!

3 lbs. chicken wings, separated
8-oz. bottle Catalina salad
   dressing

1/4 c. soy sauce
2 t. fresh ginger, peeled
   and minced

Place chicken wings in a large plastic zipping bag; set aside. Combine remaining ingredients; pour over wings. Seal bag and refrigerate several hours to overnight. Drain; bring marinade to a boil in a small saucepan. Place wings on a broiler pan. Broil for about 20 minutes, turning once, until chicken juices run clear. Brush occasionally with marinade. Makes about 3 dozen.

Teriyaki Chicken Wings

Beth Bundy
Long Prairie, MN

Line your baking sheet with aluminum foil for no sticky clean-up!

3 lbs. chicken wings, separated
3 T. soy sauce
2 T. brown sugar, packed

2 T. oil
1/2 t. ground ginger
1/4 t. garlic powder

Place chicken wings in a large plastic zipping bag. Mix together remaining ingredients; pour over wings. Seal bag and refrigerate overnight or up to 2 days. Drain; discard marinade. Arrange wings on an aluminum foil-lined baking sheet. Bake at 350 degrees for one hour, or until chicken juices run clear. Makes about 3 dozen.

Serving saucy, sticky party foods? Fill a mini slow cooker set on low with dampened, rolled-up fingertip towels. Guests will appreciate your thoughtfulness!

Southwestern Layered Bean Dip

Cheryl Westover
Stanton, CA

My grandmother used to make this delicious dip for the whole family on outings, Girl Scout campfires with me and other events. We all love it so much. Even though Grandma has been gone for many years, her recipes live on forever in our hearts and minds.

16-oz. can spicy or mild refried
    beans
15-oz. can black beans, rinsed
1/2 c. salsa
1/4 c. pickled jalapeño peppers,
    drained and chopped
4 green onions, sliced
1/2 t. chili powder
1/2 t. ground cumin
1 c. shredded Cheddar or
    Monterey Jack cheese
1/2 c. sour cream
Garnish: chopped romaine
    lettuce, tomato, avocado,
    sliced black olives
tortilla chips

In a bowl, combine refried beans, black beans, salsa, jalapeños, onions and seasonings. Transfer to a shallow 2-quart microwave-safe dish; sprinkle with cheese. Microwave on high until beans are heated through and cheese is melted, 3 to 5 minutes. Spread sour cream evenly over top; sprinkle with lettuce, tomato, avocado and olives, as desired. Serve with tortilla chips. Serves 10 to 12.

A container of sour cream will stay fresh and tasty longer if you stir in one to 2 teaspoons of white vinegar after first opening it.

Mae's Beef & Bean Dip for Nachos

April Rogers
Huntington, IN

My mother-in-law Mae gave me this slow-cooker recipe when I got married. She used to make it often when I was dating her son, who's now my husband. We really like it!

2 lbs. ground beef, browned
   and drained
2 1-1/4 oz. pkgs. taco
   seasoning mix

16-oz. can refried beans
2 8-oz. jars mild taco sauce
2 4-oz. cans diced green chiles
tortilla chips

In a 5-quart slow cooker, combine all ingredients except tortilla chips. Cover and cook on low setting for 5 hours. Serve with tortilla chips. Serves 10.

Ugly Dip

Jennifer Orme
Ashton, ID

It's not a family gathering without this favorite dip warming in a slow cooker. My mom confessed she wouldn't eat this dip for years because it didn't look very appealing. When she finally did, she loved it!

1 lb. ground pork sausage
8-oz. pkg. cream cheese,
   softened

1 c. salsa
tortilla chips

Brown sausage in a skillet over medium heat; drain. Add cream cheese and salsa to a blender; process until smooth. Add to sausage mixture in skillet; heat through over low heat. Serve warm with tortilla chips. Serves 6 to 8.

For no-stress hostessing, have food prepared before the party begins, ready to pull from the fridge or pop in the oven as guests arrive.

Really Good Guacamole

Sheryl Eastman
Wixom, MI

My husband taught me how to make this guacamole just as his mother had taught him. It's definitely a favorite at home and at work. Here's a pointer...make sure to use a glass bowl and not metal. The metal can cause guacamole to turn black.

5 roma tomatoes, finely diced
1/2 red onion, finely diced
1/2 bunch fresh cilantro,
   finely chopped
2 to 4 jalapeño or serrano
   peppers, chopped, seeds and
   veins removed, if desired

2 t. garlic, minced
5 ripe avocados, halved
   and pitted
salt to taste
1 lime, halved
tortilla chips

In a glass bowl, combine tomatoes, onion, cilantro and peppers; add garlic and set aside. Scoop avocado pulp into a separate glass bowl. With a potato masher, mash coarsely, to the consistency of mashed potatoes. Add tomato mixture; mix well. Stir in salt. Squeeze one lime half into mixture; mix well. Taste and add juice of remaining lime half, if desired. Serve with tortilla chips. Makes 8 to 10 servings.

Mashed, fresh avocado can be frozen to keep on hand for quick guacamole. Just add 1/2 teaspoon of lime or lemon juice per avocado. Mix well and spoon into a plastic zipping bag, making sure to press out all the air before sealing. Thaw in the refrigerator.

Uncle Tom's Fresh Tomato Salsa

Denise Jones
Fountain, FL

My Uncle Tom Moore sent me this recipe when I was looking for tomato salsa recipes and it is the best one I've ever tried. Whenever I make a batch, it doesn't last long. I like to make lots of jars at once so I can give some away.

2 to 3 ripe tomatoes, chopped
1 clove garlic, minced
1 Anaheim green chile, cut into
    thirds and seeds removed
3 green onions, trimmed and
    cut into 1-inch pieces
4-oz. can chopped green chiles
1/4 c. fresh cilantro, chopped

1 T. lime juice
1 t. olive oil
salt and pepper to taste
Optional: 1 to 3 jalapeño
    peppers, seeds and veins
    removed, if desired
1/4 c. ice water

In a saucepan, combine all ingredients except ice water in the order listed. Bring to a boil over medium heat. Remove from heat; stir in ice water and let stand a few minutes before serving. Keep refrigerated. Makes 6 to 8 servings.

Dear Mary,
I'm hosting a dinner party at my home - Friday, December 31st, at eight o'clock. I do hope you can come. Please call me at (Central 5 - 6407)
Sincerely,
June Swanson

Remember that happy feeling as a kid when a party invitation arrived in the mailbox? Mail out written invitations to your next get-together, no matter how informal. Your friends will love it!

Anniversary Punch

Lorrie Owens
Munford, TN

This punch was served at my grandparents' 50th wedding anniversary celebration on February 16, 1974. I don't recall if I drank any or not...I was only 4 years old at the time! This recipe was originally called Christmas Punch, but I changed the name because I found the recipe in Grandma's recipe box. It had a note at the bottom that said "Serve at anniversary party."

12-oz. can frozen lemonade
   concentrate
12-oz. can frozen orange juice
   concentrate
46-oz. can pineapple juice

4 0.13-oz. pkgs. unsweetened
   cherry drink mix
2-1/2 c. sugar
3 ltrs. ginger ale, chilled

In a punch bowl, prepare frozen juice concentrates, adding water as called for in package directions. Add remaining ingredients except ginger ale. Cover and chill. Add ginger ale a few minutes before serving. Makes 20 servings.

A large glass punch bowl is a must for entertaining family & friends. Serve up a fruity punch, a layered salad, or a sweet dessert trifle...even fill it with water and floating candles to serve as a pretty centerpiece!

Party Platters

Minty Tea Punch

Tina Wright
Atlanta, GA

On summer days, my Grandma Minnie could always be counted on to greet you with an icy glass of refreshing punch. She had a large patch of mint in her garden. I still have mint growing in my own garden at home from a cutting she gave me!

3 c. boiling water
4 tea bags
12 sprigs fresh mint
1 c. sugar, or to taste
1 c. orange juice

1/4 c. lemon juice
5 c. cold water
Garnish: additional fresh mint,
    thinly sliced lemon or orange

Add boiling water to a large heatproof pitcher. Add tea bags and mint sprigs; let stand for about 8 minutes. Discard tea bags and mint. Add sugar; stir until dissolved. Add juices and cold water; mix well. Cover and chill. Serve over ice cubes, garnished with orange or lemon slices. Makes 10 servings.

For a fruit-studded ice ring that won't dilute the punch, arrange sliced oranges, lemons and limes in a ring mold. Pour in a small amount of punch; let freeze. Repeat several times, adding punch and freezing, until mold is full. Dip mold quickly into hot water and turn out the ice ring.

Judy's Secret Cheese Ball

Judy Waskom
Seymour, IN

Whenever I take this cheese ball to a party, pitch-in or dinner, anyone who hasn't tasted it before wants to know what's in it. I joke with them and say my great-great-grandmother gave me the recipe and it's a family secret. Then I tell them...they can't believe what's really in it!

2 8-oz. pkgs. cream cheese,
   softened
3 to 4 green onions, chopped
1-oz. pkg. ranch salad dressing
   mix

4-1/4 oz. can deviled ham
   spread
8-oz. pkg. finely shredded
   Cheddar cheese
Optional: 1/2 c. real bacon bits

Combine all ingredients in a large bowl. Mix until well blended; shape into a ball. Cover and chill for one hour before serving. Makes 8 to 10 servings.

A day or two before your party, set out all the serving platters, baskets and dishes and label them..."chips & dip," "chicken wings" and so on. When party time arrives, you'll be able to set out all the goodies in seconds flat.

Aunt Maxine's Cheese Logs

Lisa Barber
Tyler, TX

My Aunt Maxine used to make this cheesy treat every year during the holiday. We all looked forward to it. She was a great cook and loved to cook during the holidays. Now my mom makes the cheese logs too...every time I take a bite, I think about my aunt.

8-oz. pkg. cream cheese,
    softened
16-oz. pkg. Colby cheese,
    shredded

1 c. chopped pecans
1 t. garlic powder
chili powder to taste

Place cheeses in the top of a double boiler. Heat over boiling water until melted; stir well. Add pecans and garlic powder; stir well until smooth. Sprinkle chili powder generously on a piece of wax paper; set aside. With your hands, shape cheese mixture into 2 logs, each 8 to 10 inches long. Roll both logs in chili powder, coating well. Wrap logs in wax paper or plastic wrap. Refrigerate overnight, or until firm. Slice and serve. Serve 8 to 10.

What good fortune to grow up in a home
where there are grandparents.

– Suzanne LaFollette

Great-Aunt Annabelle's BBQ Meatballs   *Sarah Taylor*
Manchester, IA

This simple, very delicious recipe was given to me by my Great-Aunt Annabelle. She comes from a family of wonderful cooks. I sometimes make the sauce to use in other barbecue recipes too.

1-1/2 lbs. ground beef
3/4 c. rolled oats, uncooked
1 c. milk

2 T. dried chopped onion
1-1/2 t. salt
1 t. pepper

In a large bowl, combine all ingredients. Mix thoroughly. Using your hands or a small cookie scoop, form into bite-size meatballs. Place on a lightly greased 15"x10" jelly-roll pan. Bake at 350 degrees for 10 minutes. Remove from oven; drain drippings from pan. Pour Sauce over meatballs on pan. Meatballs may also be removed to a 2-quart casserole dish before adding sauce, to saturate them better. Bake, uncovered, at 350 degrees for one hour. Makes 18 to 24 meatballs, depending on size.

Sauce:

1 c. catsup
1/2 c. brown sugar, packed
1/2 c. light corn syrup

1/2 c. water
6 T. dried chopped onion
3/4 T. Worcestershire sauce

Combine all ingredients in a saucepan. Cook over medium-low heat, stirring often, until brown sugar dissolves.

Spills are sure to happen at parties, but don't worry! Plain club soda is an instant spot remover for fresh stains. Pour a little on the spot, let set just a few seconds, then blot excess moisture.

Sausage-Cheese Balls

Belinda Burgess
Ashville, AL

*Both my grandmother and my mother made these yummy tidbits.
I can remember having them for breakfast any day of the week as
well as holidays. I have often gone back to this recipe when needing
an addition to breakfast or brunch or an appetizer.*

1 lb. ground pork sausage	1/4 c. water
2 c. biscuit baking mix	2 c. shredded Cheddar cheese

In a large bowl, combine uncooked sausage and remaining ingredients.
With your hands, mix well and form into one-inch balls. Place on a
greased baking sheet. Bake at 350 degrees for 25 minutes, or until
golden and sausage is no longer pink. Makes about 3 dozen.

Pizza popcorn is a crunchy snack that's ready in a jiffy! Combine
1/4 cup grated Parmesan cheese, 2 teaspoons each Italian seasoning
and paprika, and one teaspoon each onion powder and garlic powder.
Sprinkle over 8 cups buttered popcorn, add salt to taste and
toss to mix well.

Seafood Cocktail

MaryBeth Summers
Medford, OR

*A favorite from when my parents lived on the Southern Oregon coast.
We've been known to add Dungeness crabmeat to the mix...yum!*

6-oz. pkg. cooked halibut, flaked
6-oz. pkg. cooked salmon,
  flaked
6-oz. pkg. cooked small shrimp,
  cleaned
3 T. plus 2 t. lemon juice,
  divided
1/2 c. celery, finely diced

1/2 c. cucumber, diced
1/4 t. salt
14-oz. bottle catsup
2 t. prepared horseradish
2 t. Worcestershire sauce
2 t. green pepper, minced
Garnish: lettuce leaves,
  lemon wedges

In a bowl, combine seafood, 3 tablespoons lemon juice, celery,
cucumber and salt. In a separate bowl, combine remaining lemon juice
and other ingredients except garnish. Cover and chill both bowls. To
serve, arrange seafood mixture on lettuce leaves in 6 sherbet glasses.
Top with sauce; serve with lemon wedges. Serves 6.

Grandma Donna's Clam Dip

Kim Turechek
Oklahoma City, OK

*My mother-in-law makes this tasty old-fashioned dip every time
we visit as a family. My kids love it & named it for her.*

4 8-oz. pkgs. cream cheese,
  softened
1/4 c. Worcestershire sauce,
  or more to taste

4 6-1/2 oz. cans minced clams,
  drained and juice reserved
assorted chips

In a bowl, blend cream cheese and Worcestershire sauce. Add clams;
stir in reserved clam juice to desired consistency. Cover and chill. Serve
with assorted chips. Makes 4 cups.

Gramma Billings' Shrimp Dip

Ashley Billings
Orono, ME

This recipe was handed down from my husband's grandmother and is a much-loved family tradition!

8-oz. pkg. cream cheese,
  softened
2 T. onion, minced
1 T. mayonnaise
1 t. lemon juice

4-oz. can small shrimp, drained
  and liquid reserved
Garnish: sliced green olives
  with pimentos
corn chips

In a bowl, blend cream cheese, onion, mayonnaise and lemon juice. Fold in shrimp, reserving a few shrimp for garnish; stir in one tablespoon reserved shrimp liquid. Garnish with reserved shrimp and olives; chill. Serve with corn chips. Serves 4 to 6.

Creamy Salmon Roll-Ups

Melody Taynor
Everett, WA

Gram used to make a version of this with canned salmon. Now I've jazzed it up with smoked salmon...delicious!

1-1/2 c. cream cheese, softened
4-oz. pkg. smoked salmon,
  chopped

3 T. capers, drained and chopped
1/4 c. fresh dill, chopped
4 10-inch flour tortillas

In a bowl, combine all ingredients except tortillas; blend well. Spread filling evenly over tortillas. Roll up tortillas tightly, jelly-roll fashion. Wrap each roll in plastic wrap. Refrigerate 4 hours or overnight, until firm. Unwrap; trim ends of rolls and slice 1/2-inch thick. Makes about 3-1/2 dozen.

Does a recipe call for 1/2 cup cream cheese? That's half of an 8-ounce package, so just slice the package in half. No measuring cup needed!

Crispy Cheese Crackers

Jenny Martin
Plano, TX

This is one of our favorite cheese crackers. It is an easier version of a Cheese Straws recipe from my grandmother. I remember my mom making them for her bridge group. Now I make them for my bunko group! The recipe makes a lot, freezes well and tastes delicious.

2 c. crispy rice cereal,
    or 1 c. finely chopped nuts
8-oz. pkg. shredded Cheddar
    cheese
1 c. margarine, softened

2 c. all-purpose flour
1/2 t. salt
1/2 t. hot pepper sauce
1/8 t. Worcestershire sauce

Place cereal or nuts in a bowl; set aside. In a separate bowl, combine remaining ingredients. Mix well and roll into marble-size balls; roll in cereal or nuts to coat. Place balls on a lightly greased baking sheet; flatten gently with a fork. Bake at 350 degrees for 15 to 20 minutes, until crisp and golden. Makes about 5 dozen.

Do you have a scrumptious party recipe for a crispy snack that everyone just raves about? Send guests home with a copy of the recipe, stapled to a small plastic zipping bag filled with the snack. They'll thank you for it!

Grandma's Party Mix

Shelly Hainline
Topeka, KS

My grandmother gave the original party mix recipe her own twist many years ago. Then my mother made Grandma's version every holiday. Now I make her recipe too. Grandma always said that a recipe not shared was a recipe lost.

6 c. bite-size crispy rice cereal
   squares
6 c. bite-size crispy corn cereal
   squares
6 c. bite-size crispy wheat cereal
   squares
3 c. doughnut-shaped oat cereal
3 c. pretzel sticks or mini twists
3 c. crunchy cheese snacks

14-oz. can dry-roasted peanuts
   or mixed nuts
1 c. canola oil
1 T. Worcestershire sauce
1 t. hot pepper sauce
1 T. garlic salt
1 T. celery salt
2 t. chili powder
1 t. seasoned salt

In a large roasting pan, combine all cereals, snacks, pretzels and nuts. In a 2-cup measure, whisk together oil, sauces and seasonings. Pour half of oil mixture over cereal mixture; toss with hands to coat well. Whisk oil mixture again; pour over cereal mixture and toss again. Bake, uncovered, at 250 degrees for 1-1/4 hours; stir well every 15 minutes. Cool completely. Store in one-gallon plastic freezer bags at room temperature or in the freezer. Makes 30 cups.

Peanuts are yummy in crunchy snack mixes, but if you need to avoid them, here are some tasty substitutes to try: dried fruit bits, sunflower kernels and mini pretzel twists. Or, just omit the nuts... your snack mix will still be tasty.

Festive Sherbet Party Punch

*Gladys Kielar
Whitehouse, OH*

*This recipe started with Grandma and we always make it
for every holiday event.*

46-oz. can pineapple juice,
   chilled
46-oz. can orange juice, chilled
12-oz. can frozen lemonade
   concentrate, thawed
12-oz. can frozen limeade
   concentrate, thawed

3 ltrs. ginger ale, chilled
1 pt. orange sherbet
1 pt. lemon sherbet
1 pt. lime sherbet

Combine all juices in a large punch bowl; stir well. Cover and chill until
serving time. Just before serving, stir in ginger ale. Add scoops of
sherbet; serve immediately. Makes 8 quarts.

The next time a party guest asks, "How can I help?" be ready
with an answer! Whether it's picking up a bag of ice, setting the
table or even bringing a special dessert, friends are usually
happy to lend a hand.

Watermelon Lemonade

Bev Fisher
Mesa, AZ

This is a really refreshing beverage for hot days. My family especially loved it because their grandfather raised watermelons to sell. The recipe uses Simple Syrup...a handy way to quickly sweeten beverages, as the sugar is already dissolved.

4 c. seedless watermelon cubes	2 c. cold water
1 c. lemon juice	Garnish: fresh mint sprigs

Make Simple Syrup ahead of time; chill. Process watermelon cubes in a blender until puréed; measure out 2 cups purée. Pass through a strainer to remove any excess pulp and pour juice into a pitcher. Add lemon juice, cold water and 3/4 cup Simple Syrup; stir well. Cover and chill. Serve over ice, garnished with a sprig of mint. Makes 4 to 5 servings.

Simple Syrup:

3/4 c. water	3/4 c. sugar

Combine water and sugar in a saucepan over medium heat. Simmer, stirring often, until sugar is dissolved. Cool and chill. Refrigerate any extra syrup for later use.

Hosting a party outdoors? Keep buzzing bees out of picnic beverages. Just stitch 4 large buttons from Grandma's button box to a large doily and drape it over an open pitcher...it's that easy!

Mama Meg's Stromboli

Megan Kreplin
Coxsackie, NY

This four-ingredient snack is simple and absolutely delicious! My mom has been making Stromboli for parties for years. Now that I have started a family I am carrying on the tradition.

11-oz. tube refrigerated French
   bread dough
1/2 lb. deli ham, thinly sliced

10 to 12 slices provolone cheese
10 to 12 sandwich-size slices
   pepperoni

Lay bread dough on a greased baking sheet, seam-side up. Separate seam; unroll carefully without tearing the dough. Layer ham, cheese and pepperoni slices on dough, leaving a small border around edge. Arrange so that cheese doesn't touch the dough. Roll up dough to form a log, starting on one short edge and tucking in fillings as needed. Pinch dough to close seam; lay on baking sheet seam-side down. Bake at 425 degrees for 20 to 25 minutes, until golden. Cool on a cutting board for 5 to 10 minutes to set up; slice and serve. Makes 6 to 8 servings.

An old-fashioned galvanized washtub is perfect for chilling drinks. Fill it up with ice, then tuck in bottles of soda...they'll stay frosty all day long. Tie a bottle opener to the handle with a ribbon.

Chinese Ribs

Beth Backer
Burton, OH

This is a recipe that I learned to make from my grandmother.

5-oz. bottle soy sauce
1 c. plus 2 T. brown sugar,
   packed
1 t. garlic salt
1 lb. pork spareribs, sliced apart

1 c. catsup
1 c. water
1/4 c. Worcestershire sauce
paprika to taste

Combine soy sauce, one cup brown sugar and garlic in a plastic zipping bag. Add ribs; turn to coat. Seal bag and refrigerate 8 hours to overnight. Drain; remove ribs to a lightly greased shallow baking pan. Cover and bake at 350 degrees for 1-1/2 hours. Meanwhile, combine remaining brown sugar and other ingredients in a saucepan; simmer over low heat until sugar dissolves. Remove ribs from oven and uncover; brush sauce over ribs. Bake, uncovered, for another 30 minutes. Serves 4.

An edible centerpiece is so easy! Simply pile colorful fruit in a basket, then tuck nuts into the spaces in between. Try lemons and almonds in summer, apples and walnuts in fall.

Ranch Pretzels

Leona Krivda
Belle Vernon, PA

My grandkids look forward to munching on some of these tasty pretzels whenever they come to visit.

15-oz. pkg. hard sourdough
    pretzels, broken into small
    pieces
1-oz. pkg. ranch salad
    dressing mix

1 c. butter, melted
1/4 t. lemon pepper
1/4 t. garlic powder
1/4 t. dill weed

Place pretzel pieces in a large bowl; set aside. In a separate bowl, whisk together remaining ingredients very well; pour over pretzels. Stir to coat all pieces well. Spread on an ungreased baking sheet. Bake at 275 degrees for one hour, stirring every 15 minutes. Let cool; store in airtight containers. Makes 10 to 15 servings.

Grandma's Pull-Apart Parmesan Bread

Gladys Kielar
Whitehouse, OH

Celebrate anytime with this yummy pull-apart bread.

3 T. margarine, melted and
    divided
1/2 c. grated Parmesan cheese

10-oz. tube refrigerated
    buttermilk biscuits,
    quartered

Place melted margarine in a small bowl. Brush one teaspoon margarine over bottom and sides of an 8"x4" loaf pan; set aside. Place cheese in another small bowl. Dip biscuit pieces, one at a time, into margarine and then into cheese, coating all sides. In loaf pan, layer coated biscuit pieces with edges touching. Bake until golden, 30 to 35 minutes at 350 degrees. Let stand one minute before serving. Makes 6 servings.

Set up tables in different areas around the house so guests can mingle as they enjoy yummy spreads and finger foods.

Southern Sensation

Charleen McCarl
San Antonio, TX

This recipe has been handed down in my family in Louisiana for many years. It is a wonderful, unexpected flavor and so simple to prepare! Let a food processor do the chopping, then wait for the compliments.

1 c. green onions, finely chopped
1 c. toasted pecans, finely
    chopped
1 c. finely shredded Parmesan
    cheese

1/8 t. hot pepper sauce,
    or to taste
1/2 to 3/4 c. mayonnaise
assorted crackers or chips

In a bowl, combine onions, pecans, cheese and hot sauce. Add just enough mayonnaise to bind everything together. Transfer to a serving bowl. Cover and chill overnight for the best flavor. Serve with an assortment of crackers or chips for scooping. Makes 8 to 10 servings.

Start a kitchen journal to note favorite recipes, family preferences, even special guests and celebrations. It'll make planning meals and parties much easier and is sure to become a cherished keepsake.

Fruit Salsa Spread & Dip

Shelley Rocha
Tyler, TX

My grandmother's recipe is super easy, yet super good!

2 Granny Smith apples, peeled,
   cored and chopped
1 kiwi, peeled and chopped
1 c. strawberries, sliced, thawed
   if frozen

2 T. brown sugar, packed
2 T. apple jelly
juice of 1 orange
cinnamon graham crackers
   or vanilla wafers

In a serving bowl, combine fruit, brown sugar, jelly and juice. Mix together gently. Serve with graham crackers or vanilla wafers. Makes 8 servings.

Mom's Easy Fruit Dip

Theresa Wehmeyer
Rosebud, MO

My mom introduced me to this sweet, creamy dip
and now it's the only one I serve!

8-oz. pkg. cream cheese,
   softened
1/2 c. sugar

7-oz. jar marshmallow creme
1/8 t. nutmeg
strawberries, apple slices

In a bowl, combine cream cheese and sugar; beat to a smooth consistency. Add marshmallow creme and nutmeg; stir until combined. Serve with fruit. Keep chilled. Makes 14 servings.

Need a quick snack for the kids? Serve up an old favorite, Ants on a Log...celery sticks filled with peanut butter and sprinkled with raisins. Kids will love it!

Party Platters

Pineapple Cheese Ball

Donna Scheletsky
Baden, PA

My cousin made this yummy cheese ball for her grandmother's 90th birthday party. It's so easy and quick to whip up, using items most of us have on hand all the time.

2 8-oz. pkgs. cream cheese,
   softened
3-oz. pkg. instant French vanilla
   pudding mix

8-oz. can crushed pineapple,
   well drained
1/2 c. chopped pecans
snack crackers

Mix cream cheese, pudding mix and pineapple in a bowl. Form into a ball. Spread pecans on a sheet of wax paper; roll ball in nuts. Wrap in wax paper; chill at least one hour. Place on a serving plate; serve with crackers. Makes 10 to 12 servings.

Grandma's Peanut Butter Dip

Cindy Pogge
Kanawha, IA

This recipe is my family's favorite to dip veggie and apple slices, spread on toast...even make a peanut butter sandwich. I always have it on hand, especially at Christmas.

1 c creamy peanut butter
1 c. corn syrup
1/2 c. marshmallow creme

2 T. maple syrup
1 t. hot water

Combine all ingredients in a bowl; mix well. Keep refrigerated. Makes 2-1/2 cups.

A new way to serve your favorite dip! Just spread dip onto flour tortillas, roll up jelly-roll style and cut into one-inch slices.

Spiced Party Pecans

Mabel Davenport
Princeton, NJ

These pecans are addictive...you can't eat just one!
I have been making this recipe for over 30 years.

1 egg white
1 t. cold water
1 lb. pecan halves

1/2 c. sugar
1/4 t. salt
1/2 t. cinnamon

Beat egg white slightly; add water and beat until frothy, but not stiff. Fold in pecans. Combine sugar, salt and cinnamon. Add to pecans and mix well. Spread in a buttered 13"x9" baking pan. Bake at 250 degrees for one hour. Makes about 4 cups.

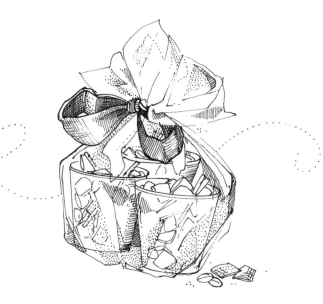

Take-home favors are sure to be appreciated. Fill clear plastic cups with crunchy snack mix or spiced nuts. Seal with sheets of colorful plastic wrap to keep the goodies inside. Heap the cups in a basket.

Scrumptious Sweet Treats

Gram's Whoopie Pies

Nadine Jones
Corinth, ME

My grandmother made these delicious creme-filled Whoopie Pies all the time when I was growing up. I made them for my children too. Now, my husband takes them to hunting camp every November. They're so popular, I always double or even triple the recipe!

2 c. all-purpose flour
1/2 c. baking cocoa
1 t. baking soda
1 t. salt
1/2 c. shortening

1 c. sugar
2 eggs, beaten
1 t. vanilla extract
1 c. milk

In a bowl, mix together flour, cocoa, baking soda and salt; set aside. In a large bowl, blend together shortening and sugar. Add eggs and vanilla; stir well. Add flour mixture alternately with milk; beat well. Drop batter by tablespoonfuls onto greased baking sheets. Bake at 350 degrees for 12 minutes, or until set and a toothpick tests done. Remove cookies from baking sheets; cool. Spread the flat side of half the cookies with Marshmallow Filling; sandwich with remaining cookies. Makes about one dozen.

Marshmallow Filling:

3/4 c. shortening
3/4 c. powdered sugar

6 T. marshmallow creme
1 t. vanilla extract

In a large bowl, combine all ingredients; beat until smooth.

A big home-baked cookie makes a sweet after-dinner treat. Place in a cellophane bag tied closed with a ribbon. Family & friends will feel extra special!

Chocolate Drop Cookies

Donna Weidner
Schaumburg, IL

Grandma always had cookies in her house, even when we stopped in on surprise visits. Of all the many, many varieties she made, these were my favorite then and they are still my favorite today!

1/2 c. butter, softened	1-1/2 t. baking powder
1 c. sugar	1-3/4 to 2 c. all-purpose flour
1 egg, beaten	1/2 c. chopped nuts
1/2 c. milk	
2-1/2 sqs. unsweetened	
baking chocolate	

In a large bowl, blend butter and sugar together. Add egg and milk; stir well and set aside. Melt chocolate according to package directions. Add melted chocolate to batter; mix well. Add baking powder and flour. Mix well and fold in nuts. Drop batter by heaping teaspoonfuls onto buttered baking sheets. Bake at 350 degrees for 10 minutes. Makes 3 dozen.

For flavor and texture when baking cookies, butter is better!
If you prefer to use margarine, though, be sure to use regular
stick margarine rather than reduced-fat margarine,
which has a higher water content.

Oatmeal Chocolate Chip Cookies

Sandy Ward
Anderson, IN

Grandma Nellie always kept her cookie jar full. Her house smelled like freshly baked cookies no matter what time you dropped in! Her secret was to use packaged cake mix for her main ingredient, then she just added to it. Everyone loved her cookies, no matter what combination she came up with.

18-1/2 oz. pkg. yellow cake mix
1 c. quick-cooking oats, uncooked
3/4 c. butter, softened

2 eggs, beaten
6-oz. pkg. semi-sweet chocolate chips
1/2 c. chopped pecans

In a large bowl, combine dry cake mix, oats, butter and eggs. Beat until well blended. Stir in chocolate chips and pecans. Drop by teaspoonfuls onto ungreased baking sheets. Bake at 350 degrees for 10 to 12 minutes, until lightly golden. Do not overbake. Cool cookies slightly on baking sheets; remove to a wire rack to cool completely. Makes 4 dozen.

When whisking ingredients in a bowl, set the bowl on
a damp kitchen towel and the bowl won't slip.

Scrumptious
Sweet Treats

Grandma Mitten's Oatmeal Cookies

Myra Mitten
Goldfield, IA

These oatmeal cookies are full of flavor and disappear quickly!

1 c. butter, softened
1 c. sugar
2 eggs, beaten
1 t. baking soda
2 T. hot water
2 c. all-purpose flour

2-1/2 c. rolled oats, uncooked
1/2 t. salt
1 t. cinnamon
1/2 t. ground cloves
1 c. raisins
Optional: 1/4 c. chopped walnuts

In a bowl, blend butter and sugar until fluffy. Add eggs and mix well. Dissolve baking soda in hot water. Add to butter mixture and mix well; set aside. In a separate large bowl, mix flour, oats, salt and spices. Add to butter mixture and mix well. Stir in raisins and nuts, if using. Drop by tablespoonfuls onto lightly greased or parchment paper-lined baking sheets. Bake at 350 degrees for about 8 to 10 minutes, until lightly golden. Makes 3 dozen.

Place a slice of soft bread in a bag of brown sugar that has hardened and seal the bag. The sugar will soften in a couple of hours.

Chinese Chews

Janis Parr
Ontario, Canada

This recipe brings back such wonderful memories of Mom and me measuring and giggling together as we made these delicious cookies. It's the first cookie that she showed me how to make. I got to measure all of the ingredients and then stir, stir, stir. They smelled heavenly while baking and tasted just as good. I still have the recipe in my little tin recipe box.

2 eggs
1 c. sugar
1/4 t. salt
1 c. chopped dates

1 c. flaked coconut
1 c. chopped walnuts
1/2 c. powdered sugar or
    superfine sugar

In a bowl, beat eggs well. Add sugar and salt; stir well. Add dates, coconut and walnuts; stir well to combine. Pour batter into a greased 2-quart casserole dish. Bake, uncovered, at 350 degrees for 30 minutes. Remove from oven; stir well and allow to cool. When cool, roll dough into small balls or logs. Coat with powdered sugar. Store in an airtight container. Makes 1-1/2 to 2 dozen.

A one-gallon glass apothecary jar makes a great cookie jar. Personalize it by using a glass paint pen to add a personal message and hearts or swirls, just for fun.

Sweet Treats

No-Bake Cookies

Becky Kuchenbecker
Ravenna, OH

These cookies taste like a cross between cookies and candy! My Grandma Gless made them often and we still love this fast, simple recipe. They're not the typical no-bake cookie as they contain no peanut butter.

3 c. quick-cooking oats, uncooked	1 t. vanilla extract
	1/2 c. milk
1 c. flaked coconut	2 c. sugar
1 c. semi-sweet chocolate chips	1/2 c. butter
1/2 c. chopped pecans	1/2 t. salt

In a large bowl, combine oats, coconut, chocolate chips, nuts and vanilla. Mix well; set aside. In a large saucepan over medium-low heat, combine remaining ingredients. Cook until butter is melted. Remove from heat. Add oat mixture; blend well. Working quickly, drop by teaspoonfuls onto wax paper-lined baking sheets or platters. Chill. Makes 3 to 4 dozen.

No-Bake Peanut Butter Cookies

Connie Harris
Friendly, WV

I can't make no-bake cookies where you cook the syrup. They are either spoon cookies or too hard to bite! But this recipe works well for me. I have been writing my recipes down for my grandchildren and I hope they enjoy them someday.

1 c. margarine	3 c. quick-cooking oats, uncooked
1/2 c. creamy peanut butter	3 c. powdered sugar

Melt margarine with peanut butter in a saucepan over low heat. Stir until blended. Add oats; stir very well. Add powdered sugar; mix well. Scoop dough by teaspoonfuls onto wax paper-lined baking sheets; cool. If desired, roll cooled cookies between your hands to make them round. Makes 2-1/2 dozen.

Grammie's Molasses Cookies

Janae Mallonee
Marlboro, MA

This recipe was handed down from my Grammie Dwinells. I have my handwritten copy (thanks, Auntie Audrey!) and it's one of the very few paper recipes I refuse to ever part with. There is just something about seeing the familiar handwriting that feels like a little hug every time I pull it out to bake these cookies.

1 c. shortening	2 t. ground ginger
1 c. sugar	2 t. baking soda
1 c. molasses	1/2 c. hot water
2 eggs, beaten	3 c. all-purpose flour
2 t. cinnamon	

In a large bowl, blend together shortening and sugar. Add molasses, eggs and spices; stir well and set aside. In a cup, stir baking soda into hot water; add to shortening mixture and blend well. Stir in flour until dough forms. Use less flour for thinner, crisper cookies; more for fluffier cookies. Drop dough by teaspoonfuls onto ungreased baking sheets. Bake at 350 degrees for 12 to 15 minutes, until golden. Makes 3 dozen.

Ask Grandma to spend an afternoon showing you how to make the delicious dessert she's always been famous for! Be sure to have a pad & pen handy to write down every step. Afterwards, you can sample it together along with cups of steamy hot tea or coffee.

Sweet Treats

Mrs. Greenfield's Overnight Walnut Cookies

Helen Thoen
Manly, IA

These cookies are so good! As a young schoolteacher during the late 1920s, my mom and other teachers stayed at Greenfield's Rooming House in Alexander, Iowa. Mrs. Greenfield must have been a wonderful cook, as Mom made the notation, "Mrs. Greenfield's recipe" on many of our family's favorites in her recipe box.

1 c. butter, softened	1 t. baking soda
2 c. brown sugar, packed	1 t. cream of tartar
2 eggs, beaten	1 c. black walnuts or other
1 t. vanilla extract	nuts, chopped
4 c. all-purpose flour	

In a large bowl, blend together butter and brown sugar. Add eggs and vanilla; stir well. Mix in flour, baking soda and cream of tartar. Fold in nuts. Form dough into rolls, about 2-1/2 inches in diameter. Wrap rolls in wax paper and refrigerate overnight. Slice dough 1/4-inch thick. Place cookies on lightly greased baking sheets. Bake at 375 degrees for 7 minutes, or until delicately golden. Makes 4 dozen.

Keep cookies fresh longer! Line the bottom of the cookie jar with crumpled tissue paper and add a slice of bread to the cookies for moisture.

Ginger Lace Cookies

*Lea Brown
Ninnekah, OK*

My kiddos love these cookies. I'm happy I was able to get the recipe from my grandmother before she passed away.

3/4 c. butter
1 egg, beaten
1 c. sugar
1/4 c. molasses
2-1/4 c. all-purpose flour
1 t. cinnamon

1 t. ground ginger
1/2 t. ground cloves
2 t. baking soda
1/2 t. salt
Garnish: additional sugar

In a large bowl, blend together butter, egg, sugar and molasses; mix well. Mixture will be stiff. In a separate bowl, stir together remaining ingredients; add to butter mixture. Mix well; form into walnut-size balls. Roll in sugar. Place on ungreased baking sheets. Bake at 375 degrees for 8 to 10 minutes. Makes 2 dozen.

Mammaw Reno's Tea Cakes

*Ramona Wysong
Barlow, KY*

I've made these for over 40 years and everybody loves them! My Grandmother Reno gave me the recipe...she said she got the recipe back in the 1940s from an 80-year-old woman. They are delicious.

2 c. shortening
2 c. sugar
6 eggs, beaten
1 T. vanilla extract

2 T. baking powder
1-1/2 t. salt
6 c. all-purpose flour

In a very large bowl, blend together shortening and sugar. Add eggs, vanilla, baking powder and salt; mix well. Gradually add flour; do not overmix. On a floured surface, roll out dough 1/3-inch thick. Cut out with cookie cutters; place on parchment paper-lined baking sheets. Bake at 375 degrees for 7 to 9 minutes; cookies should remain pale. Makes about 4 dozen.

Grandma Mary's Shortbread

Kerry McNeil
Anacortes, WA

I received this wonderful recipe 20 years ago from a dear friend who was like a grandmother to me. When my husband and I owned a bakery, we used it every spring to bake pink, yellow and violet frosted tulip cookies by the thousands for our county's annual tulip festival.

1 c. butter, softened	2 T. cornstarch
2 c. all-purpose flour	Optional: cream cheese frosting
1/2 c. superfine sugar	

Combine all ingredients except optional frosting in a medium bowl and knead to form a smooth dough. Roll out on a floured surface to 1/4-inch thick. Cut out with a cookie or biscuit cutter. Transfer to ungreased baking sheets. Bake at 275 degrees for 45 minutes; cool. Frost with cream cheese frosting, if desired. Refrigerate until set or ready to serve. Makes 2-1/2 dozen.

You're never too old for a tea party! Make iced cookies and sugar-dusted tea cakes...fill dainty teacups with soothing chamomile tea. What a delightful way to spend time with your sisters, cousins and girlfriends of all ages...and don't forget Mom and Grandma!

Honey Date Bars

Marian Buckley
Fontana, CA

When I was growing up, I always loved seeing a familiar wax paper-wrapped packet in my school lunchbox. It meant that Grammy had baked these yummy cookie bars just for me.

3 eggs, room temperature
1 c. honey
1 c. all-purpose flour
1 t. baking powder
1/2 t. salt
2 T. oil

1 T. lemon juice
1 t. vanilla extract
2 c. chopped dates
1 c. chopped walnuts
1 T. lemon zest

In a large bowl, beat eggs well. Drizzle in honey while still beating; set aside. In a separate bowl, mix flour, baking powder and salt. Add half of flour mixture to egg mixture along with oil, lemon juice and vanilla; stir well. Add dates, walnuts and lemon zest to remaining flour mixture; toss to coat and add to egg mixture. Stir until dough forms. Spread dough evenly in a lightly greased and floured 13"x9" baking pan. Bake at 350 degrees for 30 to 40 minutes, until golden. Cool in pan on a wire rack. Cut into 24 squares. Makes 2 dozen.

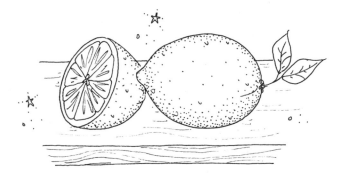

To get the most juice out of a lemon, let it come to room temperature first, then roll it on the counter with your hand. Cut lemon in half and give it a squeeze.

Grandma Ethel's Favorite Apricot Bars

Pearl Teiserskas
Brookfield, IL

I was blessed to have wonderful grandparents on both sides of the family. But Grandma Ethel was my favorite...she would plant kisses all over us and make us the most delicious desserts. Here is one that we all loved when we visited her.

1 c. butter, softened	2-1/4 c. all-purpose flour
1 c. sugar	1 c. ground pecans
1 egg, beaten	12-oz. jar apricot preserves

In a large bowl, combine butter, sugar, egg and flour. Stir in pecans. Mix with a fork until dough looks like little peas. Reserve 1-1/2 cups of dough; pat remaining dough into the bottom of a greased 13"x9" glass baking pan. Spread jam over dough; do not spread too close to the edges. Crumble remaining dough over top. Bake at 350 degrees for 40 minutes. Cut into bars. Makes 2-1/2 dozen.

A grandma is warm hugs and sweet memories. She is an encouraging word and a tender touch.

– Barbara Cage

Grandma Gloria's Chocolate Cake Brownies

Sandee Risse Yordy
Martin, SD

My mom made these every time we worked cattle on our ranch. The neighbors and relative cowhands looked forward to them! Making these now honors her good nature and her wonderful cooking.

1 c. water
1/2 c. oil
1/2 c. margarine, sliced
2 c. all-purpose flour
2 c. sugar

1/4 c. baking cocoa
1/2 c. buttermilk
1 t. baking soda
3 eggs, beaten

In a microwave-safe bowl, combine water, oil and margarine; microwave just until boiling. In a separate bowl, mix flour, sugar and cocoa. Pour water mixture into flour mixture; stir. In another bowl, combine buttermilk and baking soda; mixture will expand. Add buttermilk mixture to flour mixture; stir. Add eggs; stir. Pour batter into a greased 17"x11" baking pan. Bake at 350 degrees for 20 minutes. Cool. Pour Chocolate Frosting over cooled brownies; spread with a spatula. Cut into squares. Makes 3 dozen.

Chocolate Frosting:

1/2 c. milk
1/4 c. butter
1 c. sugar

1 t. vanilla extract
1/2 c. milk chocolate chips

In a saucepan over medium-low heat, combine milk, butter and sugar. Bring to a boil, stirring often. Boil for one minute. Remove from heat; add vanilla and chocolate chips. Beat with a rubber spatula until fairly thick.

Counting calories? Try using applesauce instead of oil in brownie recipes. Applesauce makes brownies extra moist and works just as well as oil.

Grandma's Soft Buttermilk Cookies

Nancy Kane
Ravenswood, WV

What a special treat these are...almost like little cakes! My mother was given this recipe 50 years ago by an Amish woman. My mother gave me the recipe, and I made these for my children as they were growing up. Now it has been passed to the grandchildren.

1 c. shortening
2 c. sugar
2 eggs, beaten
2 t. vanilla extract

3-1/2 to 4 c. all-purpose flour
2 t. baking soda
1/2 t. salt
1 c. buttermilk

In a large bowl, blend shortening, sugar, eggs and vanilla. In a separate bowl, mix flour, baking soda and salt. Add flour mixture to shortening mixture alternately with buttermilk; mix well. Drop by tablespoonfuls onto greased baking sheets. Bake at 400 degrees for 8 to 10 minutes. Let cookies cool on baking sheets for about a minute; remove to a wire rack. Frost with Powdered Sugar Frosting while still slightly warm. Makes 2 dozen.

Powdered Sugar Icing:

2 c. powdered sugar
1 t. vanilla extract
5 to 6 T. milk

Optional: few drops food
    coloring

Combine powdered sugar and vanilla; stir in milk to desired thickness. Add food coloring, if desired.

If an old recipe calls for a cup of sour milk, just stir a tablespoon of cider vinegar into a cup of fresh milk and let it stand for a few minutes.

Strawberry Shortcake Supreme

Becky Holsinger
Belpre, OH

I found this recipe in one of my mother's cookbooks that she's had so long it's falling apart. I copied a few recipes from the cookbook and this was one of them. I'm glad I did!

4 c. ripe strawberries, hulled and sliced	1/4 c. butter, softened
2 c. biscuit baking mix	2 egg yolks, beaten
1-1/3 c. plus 2 T. sugar, divided	1 c. sour cream
	Garnish: whipped cream

Place strawberries in a bowl; sprinkle with one cup sugar and let stand for one hour. Meanwhile, in a separate bowl, combine biscuit mix and 2 tablespoons sugar. Cut in butter with 2 knives until mixture is crumbly. Pat mixture into the bottom of an ungreased 9"x9" baking pan. Bake at 375 degrees for 10 minutes; remove from oven. In a small bowl, stir together egg yolks, sour cream and remaining sugar; spread over hot crust. Bake an additional 20 minutes. Cool completely. To serve, cut shortcake into squares and top with sweetened strawberries. Garnish with dollops of whipped cream. Makes 9 servings.

Fresh-picked berries are a special country pleasure. Store them in a colander in the refrigerator to let cold air circulate around them. Don't rinse them until you're ready to use them.

Gram's Cheesecake

Renae Hoffman
Churubusco, IN

This is a secret recipe that my Gram always made. No one in my family could make it like she did! I had baked with her since I was very little and that's how I learned how to do it. At Christmas, it brings back all the wonderful memories of Gram.

5-1/3 c. graham cracker crumbs
1/2 c. butter, melted
2 envs. unflavored gelatin
1/2 c. cold water
4 pasteurized eggs, separated
1/2 c. milk

3/4 c. sugar
1/2 t. salt
8-oz. pkg. cream cheese,
  softened
1 pt. whipping cream

Combine cracker crumbs and melted butter in a bowl; mix well. Set aside 1/4 cup of crumb mixture for topping. Press remaining mixture into the bottom and sides of a 13"x9" baking pan or two 9" pie plates; set aside. Combine gelatin and cold water in a cup; set aside for at least 10 minutes. In a saucepan, beat 4 egg yolks lightly. Add milk, sugar and salt; stir well. Cook, stirring constantly, over medium-low heat for 5 to 7 minutes. Remove pan from heat; add gelatin mixture and stir lightly. Let cool. In a separate bowl, beat cream cheese well until smooth. Add to egg mixture. In another bowl, beat cream with an electric mixer on high speed until soft peaks form. Fold into egg mixture. In a clean bowl, with clean beaters, beat egg whites on high speed until stiff peaks form. Fold into cream cheese mixture. Pour filling into pan(s). Cover and refrigerate 24 hours, or until set. At serving time, sprinkle with reserved crumb mixture. Makes 16 servings.

Eggs work best in baking recipes when they're brought to room temperature first. If time is short, just slip the eggs carefully into a bowl of lukewarm water and let stand for 15 minutes...they'll warm right up.

Grandma's Best Spice Cake

Cheryl Culver
Perkins, OK

My grandma always made the best foods. She taught me to cook when I was very young...I always enjoyed helping her. To this day, her spice cake is the best one I have ever tasted.

5-1/2 T. butter
1/2 c. plus 2 T. dark corn syrup
1/2 c. sugar
2 t. cinnamon
1 t. ground ginger
1 t. ground cardamom
1/2 t. ground cloves

1 t. orange zest
3 eggs, beaten
1-1/2 c. all-purpose flour
2 t. baking powder
1/2 c. raisins
Garnish: powdered sugar

In a saucepan over medium-low heat, bring butter, syrup, sugar, spices and zest to a boil. Cool completely. Beat in eggs, one at a time. In a separate bowl, mix flour, baking powder and raisins; fold into batter. Pour batter into a well-buttered tube cake pan. Bake at 350 degrees for one hour, or until cake tests done with a toothpick. Before serving, dust cake with powdered sugar. This cake keeps well at room temperature. Makes 8 to 10 servings.

Pantry Pan Spread

Emily Farley
Franklin, OH

This is a handy kitchen item my Grandma Farley used for greasing cake pans. She even gave away jars of it as gifts! Grandma was an amazing person who could always cheer you up. She came from the mountains of West Virginia and worked at a school as a head cook.

1/2 c. oil
1/4 c. shortening

1 c. all-purpose flour

Combine all ingredients in a bowl; beat well with an electric mixer on low speed. Store in an airtight container at room temperature. Use to grease and flour cake pans in one step. Makes about 1-1/2 cups.

Sweet Treats

Chocolate Chip-Date Cake

Renée Boyes
Wilmington, OH

My mom made this for us as kids growing up. After she passed away in 2003, I carried on the tradition...I even use Mom's original cake pan. My sisters and I think of Mom every time we eat it.

1-1/2 c. boiling water
1 c. chopped dates
1-3/4 t. baking soda, divided
1/2 c. shortening
1-1/2 c. sugar, divided
2 eggs, well beaten

1-1/2 c. all-purpose flour
1/4 t. salt
12 oz. pkg. semi-sweet
    chocolate chips
1/2 c. chopped walnuts

In a small bowl, pour boiling water over chopped dates and one teaspoon baking soda. Mix together and allow to cool. In a separate bowl, blend shortening and one cup sugar. Add eggs to shortening mixture; stir well. Add cooled date mixture; stir again. In another bowl, mix flour, salt and remaining baking soda. Combine with shortening mixture; mix well. Pour batter into a greased 13"x9" baking pan. Combine chocolate chips, walnuts and remaining sugar; sprinkle over batter. Bake at 350 degrees for 30 minutes. Cool; cut into squares. Serves 15 to 18.

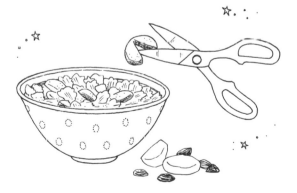

Whole pitted dates are often more flavorful than the pre-chopped variety. They're easy to chop at home using kitchen scissors.

Grandma Beach's Oatmeal Picnic Cake
Pat Beach
Fisherville, KY

I have such fond memories of my husband's mother making this cake for our family picnics at the park or at the lake for a day of fun in the sun. It's an heirloom recipe I'm sure your family will love!

1-1/4 c. boiling water
1 c. quick-cooking oats, uncooked
1/2 c. margarine
1 c. sugar
1 c. light brown sugar, packed

2 eggs, beaten
1-1/2 c. all-purpose flour
1 t. baking soda
1/2 t. salt
1-1/2 t. cinnamon
1 t. vanilla extract

In a bowl, pour boiling water over oats; set aside for 30 minutes. In a separate large bowl, blend margarine and sugars together. Add eggs and oat mixture; stir well. Add remaining ingredients; mix well. Pour batter into a greased 13"x9" baking pan. Bake at 350 degrees for 30 minutes. Spread Nut Topping over hot cake; bake an additional 10 minutes. Cut into squares. Makes 12 servings.

Nut Topping:

1/2 c. margarine, melted
1 c. brown sugar, packed
1/2 t. vanilla extract

1 c. flaked coconut
1/4 c. evaporated milk
1/2 c. chopped nuts

Mix together all ingredients until well blended.

If you see a vintage cake pan with its own slide-on lid at a tag sale, snap it up! Not only is it indispensable for toting cakes and bar cookies to parties, it also makes a clever lap tray for kids to carry along crayons and coloring books on car trips.

Peanut Butter Meltaway Cake

Julia Shenkle
Dubois, PA

When my husband and I were first married, he worked for a local funeral home. The city recorder, a very dear friend to both of us, shared this cherished family recipe with me.

1 c. water
1-1/2 c. butter, divided
6 T. baking cocoa, divided
2 c. all-purpose flour
2 c. sugar
1/2 t. salt
1 t. baking soda
2 eggs, beaten

1/2 c. sour cream
2 T. plus 2 t. vanilla extract, divided
1 c. creamy peanut butter
1 T. oil
6 T. milk
16-oz. powdered sugar

In a saucepan over medium heat, bring water, one cup butter and 3 tablespoons cocoa to a boil. Stir in flour, sugar, salt and baking soda. Add eggs, sour cream and 2 tablespoons vanilla; mix well. Pour batter into a greased 15"x10" jelly-roll pan. Bake at 350 degrees for 30 to 35 minutes, until a toothpick inserted in the center comes out clean. Cool 20 minutes. In a bowl, mix together peanut butter and oil; spread over cooled cake. In a separate saucepan over medium heat, bring milk, remaining butter and remaining cocoa to a boil. Cook and stir for 2 minutes; cool slightly. Add powdered sugar and remaining vanilla. Beat well and spread over cake. Refrigerate for 2 hours; cut into squares. Makes 15 servings.

Invite family & friends to a Sunday afternoon dessert social!
Everyone brings a pie, a cake or another favorite dessert...
you provide the ice cream and whipped cream.

Nanny's Chocolate Cupcakes

Tonya Reese
Upper Black Eddy, PA

*Every Sunday all of my aunts, uncles and cousins would have
a big Sunday dinner at Nanny and Pappy's house. The grandkids
couldn't wait to snack on Nanny's chocolate cupcakes!*

2 eggs, beaten
1 c. milk
1/2 c. oil
1 t. vanilla extract
2 c. all-purpose flour
2 c. sugar

1 t. baking powder
2 t. baking soda
1/2 t. salt
3/4 c. baking cocoa
1 c. hot brewed coffee

In a large bowl, beat together eggs, milk, oil and vanilla. Add flour,
sugar, baking powder, baking soda, salt and cocoa. Mix well; stir in
coffee. Batter will be runny. Pour batter into greased or paper-lined
muffin tins, filling 3/4 full. Bake at 350 degrees for 20 to 23 minutes,
until cupcakes test done with a toothpick. Cool; spread with Cocoa
Frosting. Makes 2-1/2 dozen.

Cocoa Frosting:

1/2 c. butter
2/3 c. baking cocoa
3 c. powdered sugar, divided

6 T. milk
1 t. vanilla extract

Beat butter, cocoa and one cup powdered sugar until creamy. Gradually
add remaining sugar and milk; beat until smooth. Stir in vanilla.

Cream-filled cupcakes! Use a melon baller to scoop out the centers
of baked cupcakes from the top. Fill with an extra dollop
of creamy frosting and top with sprinkles.

Sweet Treats

Grandma Rowland's Hickory Nut Cake

Cindy Neel
Gooseberry Patch

This recipe is my great-grandma's. She could always make a really great meal out of almost nothing. Great-Grandma Florence was a strong lady who could still touch her toes at 89 years old!

2/3 c. butter
2 c. sugar
3 eggs, separated
3 c. all-purpose flour
1 T. baking powder

1 t. salt
1 c. milk
1 c. hickory nuts, chopped
1 t. vanilla extract

In a large bowl, blend butter and sugar. Add egg yolks and beat well. Add flour, baking powder, salt and milk; mix well. Fold in nuts. In a separate bowl, beat egg whites with an electric mixer on high speed until fluffy but not stiff. Fold egg whites and vanilla into batter. Spoon batter into a greased 13"x9" baking pan. Bake at 350 degrees for 30 to 35 minutes, until a toothpick comes out clean. Cut into squares. Serves 12.

Dig into Grandma's recipe box for that extra-special dessert you remember...and then bake it to share with the whole family!

Fresh Apple Cake

Catherine Stack
Carroll, OH

This was my grandma's recipe and she always made it when we went to her house. It is my dad's favorite cake and my family's too.

1/2 c. shortening
2 c. sugar
2 eggs, beaten
2-1/2 c. all-purpose flour
2 t. baking soda
1 t. nutmeg

1 t. cinnamon
1 t. vanilla extract
4 c. cooking apples, peeled, cored and chopped
Optional: 1/2 c. chopped nuts

In a large bowl, blend together shortening, sugar and eggs. Add flour, baking soda and spices; mix well. Stir in vanilla, apples and nuts, if using. Pour batter into 10"x8" baking pan. Bake at 350 degrees for 45 minutes. Pour Brown Sugar Topping over cake while still hot. Cut into squares. Serves 10.

Brown Sugar Topping:

1/2 c. butter, melted
1/2 c. brown sugar, packed
1/2 c. sugar

1/2 c. milk
2 T. all-purpose flour

Melt butter in a saucepan over medium heat. Add remaining ingredients. Cook and stir until mixture comes to a boil.

For delicious apple pies and cakes, some of the best apple varieties are Granny Smith, Gala and Jonathan.

Mugga's Dump Cake

Jill Jones
Richmond, TX

When my son was small, he couldn't say "grandmother" so he called my grandmother "Mugga." This is a wonderful dessert she made and it always reminds me of her. Scrumptious served warm with vanilla ice cream!

11-oz. can crushed pineapple
21-oz. can apple or peach
   pie filling
1/2 c. sugar

18-1/2 oz. pkg. yellow
   cake mix
1/2 c. butter, melted

Add pineapple with juice to a greased 13"x9" baking pan; top with pie filling. Sprinkle with sugar and dry cake mix; press down with your fingers. Drizzle melted butter over top. Bake at 350 degrees for 45 minutes. Cut into squares; serve warm. Serves 12.

Strawberry Pudding Cake

Gloria Ashton
Vine Grove, KY

My great-grandmother, grandmother and mother have used this recipe. All generations just keep using this delicious recipe! Good to serve also for breakfast as a coffee cake.

1-1/2 c. sugar
2 eggs, beaten
3/4 c. oil
1 c. sour cream

1 t. baking soda
2-1/4 c. all-purpose flour
2 c. strawberries, hulled and
   sliced, thawed if frozen

In a bowl, combine sugar, eggs, oil and sour cream; mix well. Add baking soda and flour; mix well. Fold in strawberries. Pour batter into a greased and floured 13"x9" baking pan. Bake at 350 degrees for 45 minutes, or until cake tests done with a toothpick. Cool; refrigerate and serve chilled. Serves 12 to 16.

Few things are more delightful than grandchildren
fighting over your lap.

– Doug Larson

Pistachio-Pineapple Pie

Kathleen Walker
Mountain Center, CA

My great-grandmother was the ultimate baker and quilter. I loved spending weekends with her and my great-grandfather. I still remember the delicious aromas from the homemade pies as they cooled on the windowsills. This pie in its coconut crust was her particular favorite, and now my family loves it too!

1/4 c. butter, melted
2 c. flaked coconut
1-1/2 c. milk
3.4-oz. pkg. instant pistachio
    pudding mix

1 env. whipped topping mix
8-1/4 oz. can crushed pineapple,
    drained
Garnish: toasted coconut

Combine melted butter and coconut in a bowl; mix well and press into a 9" pie plate. Bake at 300 degrees for 20 minutes, or until golden. In a bowl, combine milk, pudding mix and topping mix. With an electric mixer on low speed, beat until blended. Gradually increase beating speed; beat at high speed for 5 minutes, or until thickened. Fold in pineapple. Spoon into baked crust. Cover and chill 3 hours. Garnish with toasted coconut. Makes 8 servings.

A sprinkle of toasted coconut really dresses up creamy desserts. Spread shredded coconut in a shallow pan and bake at 350 degrees for 7 to 12 minutes, stirring frequently, until toasted and golden.

No-Bake Lemon Icebox Pie

Cheri Maxwell
Gulf Breeze, FL

This was my grandmother's go-to recipe for a dessert that's cooling in summertime and not too filling at a holiday meal.

8-oz. pkg. cream cheese,
    softened
14-oz. can sweetened condensed
    milk

1/2 c. lemon juice
1 T. lemon zest
9-inch graham cracker crust
Optional: whipped cream

In a large bowl, combine all ingredients except crust and whipped cream. With an electric mixer on medium speed, beat until smooth. Spread evenly in crust. Cover and chill 4 hours, or until set. Serve with whipped cream, if desired. Serves 6 to 8.

Grannie's Banana Pudding

Mariellen Brunt
Elkton, KY

This old-fashioned, made-from-scratch recipe was handed down from my grandmother to my mother and then on to me. It has been voted "Best Banana Pudding" among my friends.

45 vanilla wafers, divided
3 ripe bananas, sliced and
    divided
3 c. milk
1-1/2 c. sugar

1/3 c. plus 3 T. all-purpose flour
2 pasteurized egg yolks, beaten
2 T. butter, sliced
1-1/2 t. vanilla extract

Set aside 10 vanilla wafers for garnish. Layer half each of remaining vanilla wafers and bananas in an ungreased 8"x8" baking pan. Cook and stir milk in a saucepan over medium-low heat until very hot; do not burn. Mix sugar and flour in a bowl. Add sugar mixture to milk; whisk continuously until mixture begins to thicken. Add egg yolks; stir well and remove from heat. Stir in butter and vanilla. Pour half of pudding over bananas. Layer with remaining wafers, bananas and pudding. Crush reserved wafers; sprinkle over top. Serve warm or chilled. Serves 8.

Grandmother's Fresh Peach Pie

Naomi Townsend
Nixa, MO

When I was growing up on the farm, we always had plenty of fresh peaches in the summertime. This recipe was a family favorite. In wintertime, you can use two 19-ounce jars of sliced peaches in syrup, drained. Decrease the sugar to 1/2 cup.

2 9-inch pie crusts, unbaked
5 c. peaches, peeled, halved,
    pitted and sliced
1 t. lemon juice

1 c. sugar
1/4 c. all-purpose flour
1/4 t. cinnamon
2 T. butter, diced

Line a 9" pie plate with one crust; set aside. In a bowl, toss together peach slices and lemon juice. In a separate bowl, stir together sugar, flour and cinnamon; mix with peaches. Turn peach mixture into pie crust; dot with butter. Cover with remaining crust. Pinch and flute edges of crust; cut several slits in crust with a knife tip. Bake at 425 degrees for 35 to 45 minutes, until crust is golden and juice begins to bubble through slits in crust. Serves 6.

Don't tuck away Grandma's beautiful cake plates, saving them for "someday." Get them out and enjoy them now! Each time they're used, they'll be a sweet reminder of her homemade treats.

Grandma Rose's Never-Fail Pie Crust
Carey Bentson
Elma, WA

On Thanksgiving, Grandma Rose's house was the place to be. Her pies were the crown jewels on the cooling rack out back, hidden from anyone wanting to take a taste or two. She loved to cook and her pie crusts were the best...always so flaky and good!

1 egg, lightly beaten	5 c. all-purpose flour
2 T. vinegar	3 c. butter-flavored shortening

Combine egg and vinegar in a one-cup measuring cup. Add enough cold water to fill the cup; set aside. Add flour to a large bowl; cut in shortening with a pastry blender or 2 knives. Blend together until shortening is well mixed into flour. Add egg mixture; stir well until dough is clumpy but not wet. Add a little more flour if needed. Divide dough into 6 to 7 rounded portions. Use immediately, or wrap well in plastic wrap; refrigerated up to 2 weeks, or freeze up to one year. Makes 6 to 7 single 9-inch pie crusts.

To use: Thaw overnight in refrigerator, if frozen. Roll out on a floured surface, about 1/4-inch thick and 12 inches in diameter. Place in a 9" pie plate. Bake according to your recipe.

For the most beautiful golden pastry crusts, use unbleached flour like Grandma did. A little beaten egg white brushed over the unbaked crust will bring out the golden color.

Honey Apple Pie

Angie Fletcher
Asheville, NC

My father's family had a stall for three generations at the Western North Carolina Farmer's Market. His mother baked and sold these apple pies every fall. I still use the very same recipe in my kitchen at home. I've found that sourwood honey is great with apples.

2 9-inch pie crusts, unbaked
6 c. Granny Smith apples, peeled
   and thinly sliced
3/4 c. honey
1/4 c. all-purpose flour

1/2 t. cinnamon
1/2 t. nutmeg
2 T. butter, diced
1/2 c. whipping cream

Line a 9" pie plate with one crust; set aside. In a large bowl, toss apple slices with honey to coat well. Add flour and spices; mix well. Spoon into crust; dot with butter. Cover with top crust. Flute or pinch edges to seal and make 6 slits in the top crust to vent steam. Cover fluted edge with a thin strip of aluminum foil. Bake at 425 degrees for 40 minutes. Remove foil strip. Very slowly and carefully pour cream into the vents. Return to oven; bake 5 minutes more. Allow to cool 10 minutes before slicing. Serves 8.

Make a sweet treat while waiting for the pie to bake. Twist scraps of remaining pie crust and roll in a mixture of cinnamon & sugar. Bake at 350 degrees for 10 minutes. So quick & easy!

Scrumptious
Sweet Treats

Mama's Butterscotch Pie

Norma Renaud
Ontario, Canada

My mom made this pie for all nine of us children, especially for my older sister who helped Mama with the care of all of us. It is delicious and special to my heart. I make it for my children and grandchildren and it is still a hit.

1/4 c. butter, sliced
3/4 c. brown sugar, packed
1-1/2 c. milk, warmed
5-1/2 T. all-purpose flour
1/2 t. salt

2/3 c. cold milk
2 eggs
9-inch pie crust, baked
Garnish: whipped cream

Cook butter and brown sugar in a saucepan over medium-low heat for 3 to 4 minutes. Stirring constantly with a whisk, add warm milk; simmer until sugar is dissolved. In a separate bowl, stir together flour, salt and cold milk. Add to hot mixture over medium heat; cook for 15 minutes. Beat eggs in a small bowl; add a small amount of hot mixture and whisk well. Gradually add egg mixture to hot mixture. Cook and stir for 2 to 3 minutes over low heat, until thickened. Pour into baked pie crust; cool completely. If desired, garnish slices with a dollop of whip cream. Makes 6 to 8 servings.

To pre-bake a pie crust, first pierce the sides and bottom thoroughly with a fork. Bake at 475 degrees until golden, 8 to 10 minutes. Allow to cool before spooning in the filling.

209

Mom's Coconut Pies

Linda Shively
Hopkinsville, KY

My mom was famous for pies, especially her coconut pies. Her whole family always called her "Pie" and I thought it was because of her cooking skills. I was grown and married before I found out that she was called "Little Pie Face" when she was a baby and that's where "Pie" came from!

1-1/2 c. sugar	1 t. vanilla extract
6 T. cornstarch	1 T. butter
6 egg yolks	2 to 4 T. flaked coconut, divided
12-oz. can evaporated milk	2 9-inch pie crusts, baked
2 c. whole milk	

In a saucepan over medium heat, combine sugar, cornstarch, egg yolks and milks. Cook over medium heat until thickened, stirring often. Remove from heat; add vanilla, butter and one to 2 tablespoons coconut. Pour filling into 2 baked pie crusts. Top pies with Meringue, spreading to edges of crust. Sprinkle with remaining coconut. Broil Meringue under oven broiler set on high, watching very closely and rotating once until evenly golden. Cool completely. Makes 2 pies; each serves 6 to 8.

Meringue:

6 egg whites	6 T. sugar, divided
1/4 t. cream of tartar	

With an electric mixer on high speed, beat egg whites and cream of tartar until soft peaks form. Continue beating and add sugar, one tablespoon at a time, until stiff peaks form.

Spreading meringue so it touches the edges of the pie crust is the secret to keeping meringue from shrinking... works every time!

Scrumptious
Sweet Treats

Skillet Cherry Pie

Pearl Teiserskas
Brookfield, IL

I used to make this quick cherry pie to take to our church socials.
It literally takes five minutes to prepare and is oh-so good!

1/4 c. butter
1/2 c. brown sugar, packed
2 9-inch frozen pie crusts,
    unbaked
15-oz. can tart cherries, drained

21-oz. can cherry pie filling
1/4 c. sugar
1 T. plus 1/8 t. all-purpose flour
1 to 2 T. milk
Optional: powdered sugar

In a cast-iron skillet, melt butter with brown sugar over medium-low
heat. Remove from heat. Place one frozen pie crust in skillet on top of
butter mixture; set aside. In a bowl, mix cherries and pie filling; spoon
into crust. Mix sugar and flour together in a cup; sprinkle evenly over
cherry mixture. Place remaining frozen pie crust upside-down on top
of cherry mixture. Brush with milk; cut slits in crust to vent. Bake at
350 degrees for one hour, or until bubbly and crust is golden. Cool;
sprinkle with powdered sugar, if desired. Serves 8.

Cherrie-O Cream Cheese Pie

Christina Rodgers
El Paso, TX

My grandmother made this yummy pie for every holiday
and every special occasion. It is so easy and so good!

8-oz. pkg. cream cheese,
    softened
14-oz. can sweetened condensed
    milk
1/3 c. lemon juice

1 t. vanilla extract
9-inch graham cracker crust
21-oz. can cherry or blueberry
    pie filling

Combine cream cheese and condensed milk in a bowl. Beat with an
electric mixer on high speed until creamy. Add lemon juice; stir until
well blended. Stir in vanilla; pour into crust. Cover and refrigerate
for 2 to 3 hours, until set. Just before serving, top with pie filling.
Serves 6 to 8.

Granny's Easy Apple Cobbler

Peggy Martinez
Wildwood, FL

This recipe has a special place in my heart, since it was taught to me by my Granny who is Heaven now. It was a real go-to recipe for our family gatherings, or just for a super-easy dessert after dinner!

1/2 c. butter, melted
1 c. self-rising flour
1 c. sugar
1 c. milk

1 t. cinnamon
2 21-oz. cans apple or
   cherry pie filling
Optional: vanilla ice cream

Pour melted butter into a 9"x9" baking pan. Mix flour, sugar and cinnamon in a bowl. Add milk; whisk until smooth. Pour batter into pan; do not stir. Add pie filling over batter by large spoonfuls. Bake at 350 degrees for 30 minutes, or until golden. Serve warm, topped with a scoop of ice cream, if desired. Serves 8 to 10.

Anna Mae's No-Fail Peach Cobbler

Rebecca Waldron
Carlyle, IL

This is a Great Depression recipe handed down through our enormous "Ann Clan." Grandma Ann used to make this when certain foods were scarce, or rationed due to the war. I would love to share its gooey goodness with you!

1/2 c. butter, melted
1 c. sugar
1 c. self-rising flour

1 c. milk
15-oz. sliced peaches, drained
   and juice reserved

Pour melted butter into a 9"x9" baking pan. In a bowl, mix together sugar, flour and milk until smooth. Pour batter into pan. Spoon peaches on top; carefully pour reserved peach juice over batter. Do not stir. Peaches will fall to the bottom and a crust will form. Bake at 350 degrees for 30 minutes, or until golden. Serves 9.

Blueberry Poor Man's Pudding

Cindy Jamieson
Ontario, Canada

This recipe was handed down from my grandmother. We are French Canadian and this is a traditional dessert. She always made it when we'd visit and I'm so glad she passed the recipe on to my mother, who has now shared it with me.

3 c. blueberries, thawed if frozen
1-3/4 c. sugar, divided
1/3 c. butter, melted
1/2 t. vanilla extract
1-1/2 c. all-purpose flour
2 t. baking powder
1/4 t. salt
1/2 c. milk, or more as needed
Optional: light cream or vanilla
    ice cream

In an 8"x8" baking pan, mix blueberries with one cup sugar; set aside. In a bowl, combine melted butter, remaining sugar and vanilla. Add flour, baking powder and salt; stir in milk until a smooth batter forms. Add more milk if batter is too thick. Pour batter over berry mixture; smooth out top. Bake at 350 degrees for 45 minutes to one hour, until a toothpick inserted deeply into center of pudding comes out clean. If top begins to get too dark, cover with aluminum foil for remaining bake time. Serve warm, garnished as desired. Makes 6 to 8 servings.

Easy Blackberry Cobbler

Irene Robinson
Cincinnati, OH

My granddaughter and I love to make this cobbler together. It's a real winner! Serve with ice cream or whipped cream...yum!

4 c. blackberries
1 T. lemon juice
1 c. all-purpose flour
1 c. sugar
1 egg, beaten
6 T. butter, melted

Place blackberries in a greased 8"x8" baking pan. Sprinkle with lemon juice; set aside. In a bowl, combine flour, sugar and egg; stir until mixture resembles coarse meal. Sprinkle over berries. Drizzle with butter. Bake at 375 degrees for 35 minutes, or until bubbly and golden. Serve warm. Makes 6 to 8 servings.

Feather Pudding

Barbara Cadwell
The Dalles, OR

A pudding baked in coffee mugs...what could be more fun? This recipe is one of my kids' favorites. My mother, their grandmother, used to make it for them when they came to visit her. It brings back wonderful memories whenever I serve it. We like to make a hole in the center and pour milk into it.

1/2 c. favorite jam	1 c. all-purpose flour
1 T. butter	2 t. baking powder
1/2 c. sugar	2-1/4 c. water, divided
1 egg, beaten	1/2 t. vanilla extract

Spray the insides of 4 heatproof coffee mugs with non-stick vegetable spray. Add 2 tablespoons jam to each mug; set aside. In a bowl, mix together butter and sugar. Add egg; beat well. In a separate bowl, combine flour and baking powder; add to butter mixture. Add 3/4 cup water and vanilla; stir well. Divide batter among mugs, filling about 1/2 full. Pour remaining water into a large saucepan; bring to a boil over medium-high heat. Carefully set the mugs into the water. Cover pan; reduce heat to medium-low and steam mugs for 30 minutes. Serve pudding warm or cold. Makes 4 servings.

Vanilla extract is a must in all kinds of baked treats!
Save by purchasing a large bottle of vanilla at a club store.
Ounce for ounce, it's much cheaper than buying the tiny
bottles sold in the supermarket baking aisle.

Homemade Chocolate Pudding

Susan Kruspe
Hall, NY

This recipe was handed down from my great-grandmother. When I was growing up on a dairy farm, with lots of milk available, my mother made this as an after-school treat. The warm pudding was such a nice welcome when we got off the school bus. A double batch would find its way into a chocolate pudding pie topped with real whipped cream, skimmed from the top of the fresh milk.

1 c. sugar	1 t. vanilla extract
1/4 c. baking cocoa	4 c. whole milk
1/4 c. cornstarch	Garnish: whipped cream
1/2 t. salt	

In a 2-quart saucepan, blend sugar, cocoa, cornstarch and salt. Add milk; stir to mix well. Cook over medium heat, stirring constantly, until thick and bubbly. Reduce heat to medium-low; cook and stir 2 minutes more. Remove from heat. Stir in vanilla. Pour pudding into individual serving dishes. Serve warm or cold, topped with a dollop of whipped cream. Makes 4 to 6 servings.

Dollops of whipped cream on a warm homemade dessert...
a perfect meal ending! In a chilled bowl, with chilled beaters,
beat a cup of whipping cream on high speed until soft peaks
form. Stir in 2 teaspoons sugar and 2 teaspoons vanilla extract.

Refrigerator Cake

Geraldine Bryant
Albuquerque, NM

My grandmother used to make this mouthwatering dessert for special occasions. This used to be her "secret recipe"...but what better way to preserve her memory than by sharing it with others? She passed away before I was born and I never met her, but I feel like I have just by eating this wonderful and simply delicious dessert.

2 16-oz. containers frozen
   whipped topping, thawed
2 11-oz. pkgs. vanilla wafers,
   crushed

12 to 14 ripe bananas, sliced
6-oz. jar maraschino cherries,
   drained
16-oz. pkg. walnut pieces

Spread a layer of whipped topping in a deep 13"x9" glass baking pan. Add a layer of crushed wafers and a layer of banana slices, with sides touching each other. Repeat until all topping, wafers and bananas are used, ending with a layer of topping. Decorate with maraschino cherries, making about 7 rows of 3 to 4 cherries each. Sprinkle walnut pieces over the top, between the cherries. Cover and refrigerate overnight. Slice in squares to serve. Makes 12 servings.

Stock up on ice cream flavors, nuts and toppings...
spend an afternoon making banana splits
(and memories) with the kids!

Grandma's Mint Dessert

Beth Richter
Canby, MN

This dessert is such a special treat! Every Easter we looked forward to Grandma's Mint Dessert...it didn't matter how full we stuffed ourselves because we always made sure to save room for dessert. Now that Grandma is gone, we still make her dessert because it's our yearly treat. We can't have Easter without it!

1 pt. whipping cream
10-1/2 oz. pkg. pastel or white
   mini marshmallows
1 c. pastel mini after-dinner
   mints, crushed

16 graham crackers, crushed
   and divided

In a deep bowl, with an electric mixer on high speed, whip cream until soft peaks form. Stir in marshmallows and crushed mints. Spread crushed graham crackers in a 13"x9" baking pan, saving 2 handfuls to sprinkle over the top. Spread whipped cream mixture over cracker crumbs in pan. Sprinkle reserved cracker crumbs over the top. Cover and chill before serving. Serves 16.

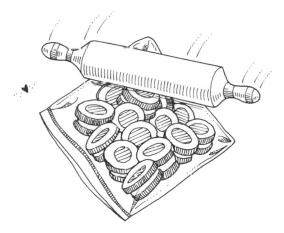

When a recipe calls for crushed crackers, cookies or cereal, place it in a plastic zipping bag and seal. Roll with a heavy rolling pin until crushed into crumbs No mess to clean up!

INDEX

INDEX

INDEX

Find Gooseberry Patch
wherever you are!

www.gooseberrypatch.com

Call us toll-free at 1·800·854·6673

U.S. to Metric Recipe Equivalents

Volume Measurements

1/4 teaspoon	1 mL
1/2 teaspoon	2 mL
1 teaspoon	5 mL
1 tablespoon = 3 teaspoons	15 mL
2 tablespoons = 1 fluid ounce	30 mL
1/4 cup	60 mL
1/3 cup	75 mL
1/2 cup = 4 fluid ounces	125 mL
1 cup = 8 fluid ounces	250 mL
2 cups = 1 pint =16 fluid ounces	500 mL
4 cups = 1 quart	1 L

Weights

1 ounce	30 g
4 ounces	120 g
8 ounces	225 g
16 ounces = 1 pound	450 g

Oven Temperatures

300° F	150° C
325° F	160° C
350° F	180° C
375° F	190° C
400° F	200° C
450° F	230° C

Baking Pan Sizes

Square		Loaf	
8x8x2 inches	2 L = 20x20x5 cm	9x5x3 inches	2 L = 23x13x7 cm
9x9x2 inches	2.5 L = 23x23x5 cm	Round	
Rectangular		8x1-1/2 inches	1.2 L = 20x4 cm
13x9x2 inches	3.5 L = 33x23x5 cm	9x1-1/2 inches	1.5 L = 23x4 cm